EASY AFGHANS *for*
KNITTERS ™

Edited by Jeanne Stauffer

Exclusively using Plymouth yarns

HOUSE of
WHITE
BIRCHES
PUBLISHERS
SINCE 1947

Easy Afghans for Knitters

Copyright © 2005 House of White Birches,
Berne, Indiana 46711

Editor: Jeanne Stauffer
Art Director: Brad Snow
Publishing Services Manager: Brenda Gallmeyer

Associate Editor: Dianne Schmidt
Assistant Art Director: Nick Pierce
Copy Supervisor: Michelle Beck
Copy Editor: Mary Martin
Technical Editor: Diane Zangl
Technical Artist: Nicole Gage

Graphic Arts Supervisor: Ronda Bechinski
Book Design: Karen Allen
Graphic Artists: Debby Keel, Edith Teegarden
Production Assistants: Cheryl Kempf, Marj Morgan

Photography: Tammy Christian, Carl Clark,
Christena Green, Matthew Owen
Photography Stylist: Tammy Nussbaum

Chief Executive Officer: John Robinson
Publishing Director: David McKee
Editorial Director: Vivian Rothe
Marketing Director: Dan Fink

Printed in China
First Printing: 2005
Library of Congress Control Number: 2004113511
Hardcover ISBN: 1-59217-069-2
Softcover ISBN: 1-59217-070-6

Retail outlet owners and resellers: For additional
copies of this book call (800) 772-6643.

Welcome!

There are 67 afghans in this book, but Plymouth Yarn Company has so many delicious yarns that we had a difficult time deciding which yarn to use for which afghan. Included are throws, lap afghans, baby blankets, kids' afghans and lots of cozy afghans to offer comfort to whoever is wrapped up in them. For those who like the unusual, we included afghans with an "arty" look. This was really easy to do with all the unique novelty yarns available from Plymouth.

A friend of mine said that she knits afghans all year long, donating them to charities who give them to new mothers or to families in crisis situations. Another friend is making a throw for every member of her family. A third friend always keeps knitted afghans on hand, ready to give as a gift for any special occasion. Everyone is knitting afghans! It's amazing how many you can make when you knit just a little every day. And when you start with fun yarns, afghans are finished faster than ever.

Once you start knitting with all the wonderful Plymouth yarns, you, too, will soon have plenty of afghans to use in your own home or to give away. Now that's exciting!

Warm regards,

Jeanne Stauffer

Contents

Glitzy Glamour Throw

Design by LANIE HERING

THIS THROW BEGINS AT ONE CORNER AND INCREASES TO THE CENTER. THERE, DECREASING BEGINS TO GIVE IT A UNIQUE DIAGONAL SHAPE.

Skill Level
 BEGINNER

Finished Size
Approx 50 inches square, with fringe

Materials
 Plymouth Baby Alpaca Grande 100 percent baby alpaca bulky weight yarn (110 yds/100g per skein): 9 skeins plum #2213 (MC)

 Plymouth Eros Glitz 86 percent nylon/10 percent rayon/4 percent Lurex medium weight novelty yarn (158 yds/50g per ball): 2 balls grapevine #104 (A)

• Plymouth Dazzlelash 78 percent polyester/22 percent rayon bulky weight eyelash yarn (220 yds/50g per ball): 1 ball grape #104 (B)

• Size 11 (8mm) 29-inch circular needle or size needed to obtain gauge

Gauge
12 sts and 22 rows = 4 inches/10cm in garter st
To save time, take time to check gauge.

Pattern Stitch
Stripes
Working in garter st, work [2 rows CC, 4 rows MC] twice, 2 rows CC.

Pattern Notes
Circular needle is used to accommodate large number of sts. Do not join; work in rows.
One strand each of A and B are held tog throughout throw. This is referred to as CC in pattern instructions.

Throw
With MC, cast on 2 sts. Knit 1 row.
Rows 1 (RS)–13: Knit in front and back of first st, knit to end of row.
Row 14: Knit in front and back of first st, knit to last 2 sts, knit in front and back of next st, k1.
Rep Rows 1–14, working in color pat of 16 rows MC, 14 rows stripe pat, [24 rows MC, 14 rows stripe pat] 3 times, 24 rows MC, 7 rows stripe pat.
This is widest part of throw.

Beg dec shaping
Rows 1–13: K2tog, knit to end of row.
Row 14: K2tog, knit to last 2 sts, k2tog.
Rep Rows 1–14, working in color pat of rem 7 rows of stripe pat, [24 rows MC, 14 rows stripe pat] 4 times, 16 rows MC.
Bind off rem 2 sts.

Fringe
Cut 12-inch lengths of all yarns.
Holding 1 strand of each yarn tog, fold group in half and attach at 2-inch intervals on all 4 sides of throw. ■

Loopy Stripes

Design by GAYLE BUNN

CUDDLE UNDER AN ULTRA-COZY AFGHAN WORKED IN A
COMBINATION OF MOHAIR AND CHUNKY WOOL YARNS.

Skill Level

 INTERMEDIATE

Finished Size

Approx 53 x 65 inches

Materials

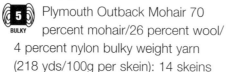 Plymouth Outback Mohair 70
percent mohair/26 percent wool/
4 percent nylon bulky weight yarn
(218 yds/100g per skein): 14 skeins
Monet #801 (MC)

Plymouth Encore Chunky 75
percent acrylic/25 percent wool
bulky weight yarn (143 yds/100g per
ball): 4 balls storm #670 (CC)

- Size 11 (8mm) 29-inch circular needle
  or size needed to obtain gauge

Gauge

10 sts and 14 rows = 4 inches/10cm in
St st with 1 strand each MC and CC
held tog
To save time, take time to check gauge.

Special Abbreviation

ML (Make Loop): Knit into next st, but do
not drop st from LH needle. Bring yarn to
front of work between needles and make
a lp around right thumb. Take yarn to back
of work between needles. Slip st on RH
needle back to LH needle (lp is between 2
sts on LH needle). K2 sts of LH needle tog,
remove lp from thumb.

Pattern Notes

Afghan is worked lengthwise.
Circular needle is used to accommodate
large number of sts. Do not join; work
in rows.

Afghan

With 2 strands of MC held tog, loosely cast
on 146 sts.
**Row 1 (RS): *ML, k1; rep from *
across row.
Row 2: Knit.
Row 3: *K1, ML; rep from * across row.
Row 4: Knit.
Rep these 4 rows until lp section measures
approx 10½ inches, ending with Row 1
of pat.***
Next row (WS): With 1 strand each of MC
and CC held tog, purl, inc 16 sts evenly.
(162 sts)
Beg and end with a knit row, work even in
St st for 10½ inches.
Next row (WS): With 2 strands of MC
held tog, purl, dec 16 sts evenly. (146 sts)**
Rep from ** to ** once, then from **
to *** once.
Loosely bind off knitwise on WS.

Edging

With RS facing and 1 strand each of MC
and CC held tog, pick up and knit 130 sts
evenly along short edge of afghan.
Loosely bind off knitwise on WS.
Rep along opposite short edge. ∎

8

EASY AFGHANS FOR KNITTERS

Seaside Sunset Throw

Design by ANITA CLOSIC

SHADES OF ROYAL PURPLE CAPTURE THE FEELING OF THE LAST SUNSET RAYS AT THE BEACH. AN ADDED BONUS: THE THROW IS REVERSIBLE.

Skill Level

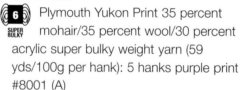 BEGINNER

Finished Size

Approx 42 x 48 inches

Materials

- **6 SUPER BULKY** Plymouth Yukon Print 35 percent mohair/35 percent wool/30 percent acrylic super bulky weight yarn (59 yds/100g per hank): 5 hanks purple print #8001 (A)
- **5 BULKY** Plymouth Odyssey Glitz 60 percent nylon/37 percent wool/3 percent lamé bulky weight novelty yarn (66 yds/50g per ball): 5 balls purple variegated #923 (B)
- **6 SUPER BULKY** Plymouth Yukon 35 percent mohair/35 percent wool/30 percent acrylic super bulky weight yarn (59 yds/100g per ball): 4 balls purple #578 (C)
- Plymouth Dazzlelash 78 percent polyester/22 percent rayon bulky weight novelty yarn (220 yds/50g per ball): 2 balls purple metallic #104 (D)
- Size 15 (10mm) 32-inch circular needles or size needed to obtain gauge

Gauge

8 sts and 10 rows = 4 inches/10cm in Fancy pat
To save time, take time to check gauge.

Pattern Stitch

Fancy

Rows 1–4: With A, knit.

Row 5: With B, knit.

Rows 6–8: With B, k2, *yo, k2tog; rep from * to last 2 sts, k2.

Rows 9–12: With 1 strand each of C and D held tog, knit.

Row 13: With B, knit.

Rows 14–16: Rep Row 6.

Rep Rows 1–16 for pat.

Pattern Notes

Circular needle is used to accommodate large number of sts. Do not join; work in rows.

Slight scallop edge forms automatically along sides of throw.

Throw

With A, loosely cast on 84 sts.

Work even in Fancy pat until 8 reps have been completed.

With C, knit 4 rows.

Bind off loosely. ∎

Fingerpaint Fun

Design by EDIE ECKMAN

CHUNKY YARN AND VARIEGATED COLORS CREATE A
SNUG AFGHAN THAT MAY REMIND YOU OF A CHILD'S
FINGERPAINT DRAWING.

Skill Level

 EASY

Finished Size

Approx 48 x 52 inches

Materials

- Plymouth Handpaint Wool 100 percent wool super bulky weight yarn (60 yds/100g skein): 14 skeins Santa Fe #160
- Size 17 (12.75mm) 29-inch circular needle
- Size 15 (10mm) double-pointed needles (2 only)

Gauge

8 sts and 11 rows = 4 inches/10cm in Double Moss pat
To save time, take time to check gauge.

Pattern Stitch

Double Moss (multiple of 4 sts)
Rows 1 and 2: *K2, p2; rep from * across row.
Rows 3 and 4: *P2, k2; rep from * across row.
Rep Rows 1–4 for pat.

Afghan

Cast on 86 sts.
Work even in Double Moss pat until afghan measures 50 inches.
Bind off loosely.

I-Cord Edging

With dpn, cast on 3 sts.
Insert needle into edge of afghan and pull up a st. (4 sts on RH needle)
Do not turn; slide sts to opposite end of needle.
*K2, k2tog-tbl, pick up and knit another st from edge of afghan. Rep from * picking up sts evenly along edge to first corner.
Unattached row: [K3, slide sts to opposite end of needle] twice.
Continue working attached I-cord along edges and unattached I-cord in corner sts around entire afghan.
Sew last 3 sts to cast-on sts. ■

Retro 1930s Boudoir Throw

Design by ANITA CLOSIC

RECAPTURE THE PAST WITH A SOFTLY ROMANTIC THROW IN SERENE COLORS.

Skill Level
◼◻◻◻ **EASY**

Finished Size
Approx 42 x 48 inches

Materials
- **5 BULKY** Plymouth Sinsation 80 percent rayon/20 percent wool bulky weight yarn (38 yds/50g per ball): 6 balls cream #3301 (A)
- **6 SUPER BULKY** Plymouth Parrot 100 percent nylon super bulky novelty yarn (28 yds/50g per ball): 5 balls ivory #43 (B)
- **6 SUPER BULKY** Plymouth Yukon 35 percent mohair/35 percent wool/30 percent acrylic super bulky weight yarn (59 yds/100g per ball): 5 balls pink #959 (C)
- Size 15 (10mm) 32-inch circular needle or size needed to obtain gauge
- Stitch markers

Gauge
8 sts and 11 rows = 4 inches/10cm in 1930s Fan pat
To save time, take time to check gauge.

Pattern Notes
Circular needle is used to accommodate large number of sts. Do not join; work in rows.

Place markers between each pat rep.

Pattern Stitch
1930s Fan (Multiple of 17sts + 4)
Rows 1 (RS)–4: With A, knit.
Row 5: With C, k2, *[k2tog] 3 times, [yo, k1] 5 times, yo, [k2tog] 3 times; rep from * to last 2 sts, k2.
Row 6: With C, k2, purl to last 2 sts, k2.
Rows 7–12: [Rep Rows 5 and 6] 3 times.
Rows 13–16: With A, knit.
Rows 17–20: With B, knit.
Rows 21–24: With A, knit.
Rep Rows 1–24 for pat.

Throw
With B, loosely cast on 89 sts.
Knit 4 rows.
Work even in 1930s Fan pat until 6 full reps have been completed.
Rep Rows 1–20.
Bind off loosely with B. ◼

Snazzy Spazzini Throw

Design by EDIE ECKMAN

SNAPPY, JAZZY, STYLISH—WHATEVER WORD YOU USE,

THIS QUICK THROW IS SURE TO GET ATTENTIVE STARES.

Skill Level
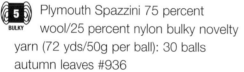 **EASY**

Finished Size
Approx 48 inches square

Materials
 Plymouth Spazzini 75 percent wool/25 percent nylon bulky novelty yarn (72 yds/50g per ball): 30 balls autumn leaves #936
- Size 15 (10mm) circular needle or size needed to obtain gauge
- 7-inch piece of cardboard

Gauge
8 sts and 16 rows = 4 inches/10cm in garter st
Exact gauge is not crucial in this project.

Special Abbreviations
M1 (Make 1): Make a backward lp and place on RH needle.

Pattern Notes
Circular needle is used to accommodate large number of sts. Do not join; work in rows.
Yarn is used double throughout. Throw is knit on the bias. If you reach the halfway point and have used more than half the yarn, rip out a row or two until half the yarn rem, and then begin dec.

Tassels
Using 1 ball of yarn, make 4 tassels each 6 inches long.
For each tassel, cut 2 strands of yarn, each 8 inches long and set aside.
Wind yarn around cardboard 25–30 times.
Using 1 reserved strand, tie one end; cut opposite end.
Wrap 2nd strand around tassel, about 1 inch below fold.
Tie tightly and hide ends in tassel.
Trim ends even.
Set aside.

Throw
Cast on 3 sts. Knit 1 row.
Inc row: K1, M1, knit to end of row.
Rep this row until edge of throw measures 48 inches.
Knit 3 rows even.
Dec row: K2tog, knit to end of row.
Rep this row until 3 sts rem.
Bind off.

Assembly
Attach 1 tassel to each corner of throw. ■

Alpaca Jewels

Design by KENNITA TULLY

DOTS OF COLOR SHINE OUT LIKE JEWELS ON A SOFT ALPACA THROW.

Skill Level
■■□□ EASY

Finished Size
Approx 40 x 40 inches

Materials
- **5 BULKY** Plymouth Alpaca Brush 80 percent baby alpaca/20 percent acrylic bulky weight yarn (110 yds/50g per ball): 7 balls kiwi #1477 (MC)
- **4 MEDIUM** Plymouth Eros Glitz 86 percent nylon/10 percent rayon/4 percent lurex worsted weight novelty yarn (158 yds/50g per ball): 3 balls leaf variegated #114 (CC)
- Size 10 (6mm) 32-inch circular needle or size needed to obtain gauge
- Size I/9 (5.5mm) crochet hook

Gauge
12½ sts and 24 rows = 4 inches/10cm in pat st
To save time, take time to check gauge.

Pattern Stitch
Slip Stitch Mesh
Row 1 (RS): With MC, purl.
Row 2: Knit.

Row 3: With CC, k3, *sl 1 wyib, k1; rep from * to last st, k1.
Row 4: K2, *sl 1 wyif; k1; rep from * to last 2 sts, k2.
Row 5: With MC k2, *yo, k2tog; rep from * to last 2 sts, k2.
Row 6: Purl.
Rep Rows 1–6 for pat.

Pattern Notes
Circular needle is used to accommodate large number of sts. Do not join; work in rows.
Two strands of CC are held tog for entire throw.

Throw
With MC, cast on 126 sts.
Work even in Slip Stitch Mesh pat until throw measures approx 40 inches, ending with Row 2 of pat.
Bind off all sts.

Reverse Single Crochet Edging
Join MC with RS facing.
Working from left to right, work 1 rnd of sc around entire throw, making sure to keep work flat.
Join with sl st. ■

Sawtooth Stripes

Design by JOANNE TURCOTTE

NO NEED TO CARRY EXTRA COLORS IN THIS AFGHAN.

SLIP STITCHES CREATE THE SAWTOOTH DESIGN.

Skill Level

 BEGINNER

Finished Size

Throw (afghan) Instructions are given for smaller size, with larger size in parentheses. When only 1 number is given, it applies to both sizes.

Finished Measurements

Approx 40 x 50 (50 x 60) inches

Materials

 Plymouth Alpaca Bouclé 90 percent alpaca/10 percent nylon super bulky weight yarn (70 yds/50g per ball): 7 (8) balls plum #2028 (A), 9 (11) balls plum tweed #3676 (B), 5 (6) balls pumpkin #2037 (C)
- Size 10½ (6.5mm) 29-inch circular needle
- Size 11 (8mm) 29-inch circular needle or size needed to obtain gauge

Gauge

10 sts and 16 rows = 4 inches/10cm in St st with larger needles
To save time, take time to check gauge.

Pattern Stitch

Sawtooth (multiple 3 sts + 1)
Row 1: With B, k3, sl 1, *k2, sl 1; rep from * to last 3 sts, k3.
Row 2: P3, sl 1, *p2, sl 1; rep from * to last 3 sts, p3.
Rows 3–10: Work in St st for 8 rows.
Row 11: With C, k3, sl 1, *k2, sl 1; rep

from * to last 3 sts, k3.
Row 12: P3, sl 1, *p2, sl 1; rep from * to last 3 sts, p3.
Rows 13–20: Work in St st for 8 rows.
Row 21: Rep Row 1.
Row 22: Rep Row 2.
Rows 23–30: Work in St st for 8 rows.
Row 31: With A, k3, sl 1,*k2, sl 1; rep from * to last 3 sts, k3.
Row 32: P3, sl 1, *p2, sl 1; rep from * to last 3 sts, p3.
Rows 33–40: Work in St st for 8 rows.
Rep Rows 1–40 for pat.

Pattern Note

Circular needle is used to accommodate large number of sts. Do not join; work in rows.

Afghan

With smaller needle and A, loosely cast on 97 (121) sts.
Work even in garter st for 6 rows. Change to larger needle.
Work even in St st for 10 rows.
Work even in Sawtooth pat until afghan measures approx 49 (59) inches, ending with Row 40.
Change to A and knit 6 rows.
Bind off loosely.

Side Border

With RS facing, using A and smaller needle, pick up and knit 125 (150) sts along one side edge of afghan.
Knit 5 rows.
Bind off loosely.
Rep on opposite side. ■

Champagne Elegance

Design by CAROL MAY

QUIET ELEGANCE AND A REVERSIBLE PATTERN COMBINE TO CREATE AN AFGHAN THAT WIL FIT INTO ANY DECOR.

Skill Level
■□□□ BEGINNER

Finished Size
Approx 34 x 52 inches

Materials

5 Plymouth Sinsation 80 percent
BULKY rayon/20 percent wool chenille
bulky weight yarn (38 yds/50g per ball):
20 balls cream #3301
• Size 10½ (6.5mm) 29-inch circular
needle or size needed to obtain gauge

Gauge
10 sts and 12 rows = 4 inches/10cm in
pat st
To save time, take time to check gauge.

Pattern Stitch
Row 1 (RS): K2, p2, k4, *p4, k4; rep from *
to last 4 sts, p2, k2.
Row 2: Purl.
Rep Rows 1–2 for pat.

Afghan
Loosely cast on 100 sts.
Work even in pat until afghan measures
52 inches.
Bind off loosely in pat. ■

Party Swirls

Design by JOANNE TURCOTTE

CIRCULAR SHAPING CREATES A UNIQUE AFGHAN, AND EYELASH YARN ADDS TEXTURAL INTEREST.

Skill Level

◼◼◻◻ EASY

Finished Size
Approx 36 (42) inches across
Instructions are given for smaller size, with larger size in parentheses. When only 1 number is given, it applies to both sizes.

Materials
 Plymouth Fantasy Naturale 100 percent mercerized cotton worsted weight yarn (140 yds/100g per skein): 5 (6) skeins black #8990 (MC)

 Plymouth Parrot 100 percent nylon super bulky weight novelty yarn (28 yds/50g per ball): 2 balls Mardi Gras #6 (CC)

- Size 9 (5.5mm) double-pointed, 16-, 24- and 32-inch circular needles or size needed to obtain gauge
- Size 10½ (6.5mm) straight needle (1 only)
- Size L/11 (8mm) crochet hook

Gauge
16 sts and 20 rows = 4 inches/10cm in St st with MC and smaller needles
To save time, take time to check gauge.

Pattern Notes
Afghan is worked circularly from center outwards. Change to longer needles as necessary.

Afghan
With MC and dpn, cast on 14 sts.
Divide onto 3 needles, having 4 sts on each of first 2 needles, and 6 sts on 3rd.
Join without twisting, pm between first and last st.
Rnd 1: *Yo, k2; rep from * around. (21 sts)
Rnd 2 and all even-numbered rnds: Knit.
Rnd 3: *Yo, k3; rep from * around. (28 sts)
Rnd 5: *Yo, k4; rep from * around. (35 sts)
Rnd 7: *Yo, k5; rep from * around. (42 sts)
Continue to inc 7 sts every other rnd as above until afghan measures 18 (21) inches from center.
Change to CC, leave sts on smaller needle.
With larger needle, loosely bind off all sts purlwise.

Spirals
With CC and crochet hook, beg at center and work 1 sc in crossbar of each yo to outer edge.
Fasten off, leaving an end of approx 6 inches. Rep for all spirals.
Work a rnd of sc around center cast-on sts to resemble a flower.
Weave in CC ends securely. ◼

Bold Macaw Throw

Design by ANITA CLOSIC

AS BRIGHT AS THE PARROT IT IS NAMED FOR, THIS THROW WILL ADD A WILD TOUCH OF COLOR AND EXCITEMENT WHEREVER IT IS LOCATED.

Skill Level

 EASY

Finished Size

Approx 42 x 48 inches

Materials

 Plymouth Eros 100 percent nylon worsted weight novelty yarn (165 yds/50g per ball): 4 balls black #3017 (A)

 Plymouth Parrot 100 percent nylon super bulky ribbon yarn (28 yds/50g per ball): 10 balls rainbow #24 (B)

- Plymouth Colorlash 100 percent polyester carry-along eyelash yarn (220 yds/50g per ball): 2 balls gold #23 (C)

 Plymouth Fantasy Naturale 100 percent mercerized cotton worsted weight yarn (140 yds/100 g per skein): 4 skeins red #3611 (D)

- Size 11 (8mm) 30-inch circular needles or size needed to obtain gauge

Gauge

14 sts and 18 rows = 4 inches/10cm in pat st
To save time, take time to check gauge.

Pattern Stitches

Feathers (multiple of 17 sts + 4)
Row 1 (RS): K2, *[k2tog] 3 times, [yo, k1] 5 times, yo, [k2tog] 3 times; rep from * to last 2 sts, k2.
Rows 2 and 3: Knit.

Row 4: K2, purl to last 2 sts, k2.
Rep Rows 1–4 for pat.

Color Sequence (28 rows)
Knit 4 rows with 2 strands A held tog, knit 4 rows with 1 strand each B and C held tog, work 12 rows in Feathers pat with 1 strand D, knit 4 rows with 1 strand each B and C held tog, knit 4 rows with 2 strands A held tog.

Pattern Notes

Circular needle is used to accommodate large number of sts. Do not join; work in rows.

Throw

With 2 strands of A held tog, loosely cast on 123 sts.
Work even in color sequence until 8 reps have been completed. (224 rows)
Bind off loosely.

Fringe

Cut strands of A and B, each 20 inches long.
Holding 2 strands of each tog, fold each group of 4 in half.
Working along cast-on edge, insert crochet hook from WS to RS between scallops.
Pull fold of fringe through fabric. Draw ends through lp and fasten tightly.
Trim fringe evenly. ■

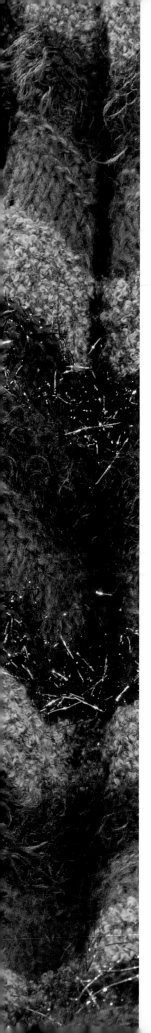

Glittering Cashmere

Design by SANDI PROSSER

SUMPTUOUS CASHMERE AND ALPACA YARNS COMBINE WITH A GLITTERY CARRY-ALONG YARN IN A VARIATION ON A CLASSIC PATTERN STITCH.

Skill Level
■■□□ **EASY**

Finished Size
Approx 44 x 55 inches (excluding fringe)

Materials

 Plymouth Royal Cashmere 100 percent fine Italian cashmere worsted weight yarn (154 yds/50g per hank): 6 hanks chocolate #344K (A)

Plymouth Alpaca Boucle 90 percent alpaca/10 percent nylon super bulky weight yarn (70 yds/50g per ball): 6 balls brown #12 (B)

Plymouth Baby Alpaca Brush 80 percent baby alpaca/20 percent acrylic bulky weight yarn (110 yds/50g per ball): 3 balls beige #1000 (C)

- Plymouth Glitterlash 50 percent polyester/50 percent metallic carry-along yarn (185 yds/25g per ball): 2 balls copper #6 (D)

Plymouth Flash 100 percent nylon worsted weight yarn (190 yds/50g per ball): 2 balls dark chocolate #993 (E)

- Size 10 (6mm) 30-inch circular needle or size needed to obtain gauge

Gauge
14 sts and 18 rows = 4 inches/10cm in Wave pat
To save time, take time to check gauge.

Special Abbreviation
CDD (Centered Double Decrease): Slip 2 sts as if to k2tog, k1, pass 2 slipped sts over knit st.

Pattern Stitches
Wave
Rows 1 and 3 (RS): K2, *yo, k6, CDD, k6, yo, k1; rep from * to last st, k1.
Rows 2 and 4: Purl.
Rows 5–8: Knit.
Rep Rows 1–8 for pat.

Pattern Notes
Circular needle is used to accommodate large number of sts.
Do not join; work in rows.

Color Stripe Sequence
Work 8 rows each of the following colors: 1 strand B, 1 strand C, 1 strand each of A and E held tog, 1 strand B, 1 strand each A and D held tog, 1 strand C, 1 strand each A and E held tog, 1 strand each A and D held tog.

Afghan

With 1 strand each of A and D held tog,
cast on 163 sts.

Knit 3 rows.

Working even in Wave pat, [rep color stripe
sequence] 4 times, ending with Row 7 of
Wave pat on final stripe.

Bind off knitwise on WS.

Fringe

Cut strands of yarn, each 18 inches long.
Holding 1 strand of each color tog, fold
each group of 6 yarns in half.

Working in each point of pat, insert crochet
hook from WS to RS.

Pull fold of fringe through fabric. Draw ends
through lp and fasten tightly.

Rep along bound-off edge.

Trim fringe evenly. ■

Contemporary Checks

Design by LOIS S. YOUNG

SOFT EYELASH SQUARES CENTERED ON TEXTURED

BLOCKS ADD A MODERN TOUCH TO A COTTON AFGHAN.

Skill Level
 EASY

Finished Size
Approx 41 x 62 inches

Materials
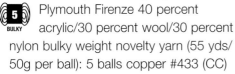 Plymouth Fantasy Naturale 100 percent mercerized cotton worsted weight yarn (140 yds/100g per skein): 12 skeins taupe #7360 (MC)

Plymouth Firenze 40 percent acrylic/30 percent wool/30 percent nylon bulky weight novelty yarn (55 yds/ 50g per ball): 5 balls copper #433 (CC)
- Size 8 (5mm) 29-inch circular needle or size needed to obtain gauge.
- Stitch holders

Gauge
16 sts and 22 rows = 4 inches/10cm in Checks pat
Each square measures 2½ inches
To save time, take time to check gauge.

Pattern Stitch
Checks
Rows 1, 3, 11 and 13 (RS): With MC, p11, *k10, p10; rep from *, end last rep p11.
Rows 2, 4, 12 and 14: With MC, k11, *p10, k10; rep from *, end last rep k11.
Rows 5, 7 and 9: P11 MC, *k3 MC, k4 CC, k3 MC, p10 MC; rep from *, end last rep p11 MC.

Rows 6, 8 and 10: K11 MC, *p3 MC, p4 CC, p3 MC, k10 MC; rep from *, end last rep k11 MC.
Rows 15, 17, 25 and 27: Rep Row 2.
Rows 16, 18, 26 and 28: Rep Row 1.
Rows 19, 21 and 23: K4 MC, *k4 CC, k3 CC, p10 MC, k3 MC; rep from *, end last rep k4 CC, k4 MC.
Rows 20, 22 and 24: P4 MC, *p4 CC, p3 MC, k10 MC, p3 MC, rep from *, end p4 CC, p4 MC.
Rep Rows 1–28 for pat.

Pattern Notes
Circular needle is used to accommodate large number of sts. Do not join; work in rows.

Use a 36-inch length of CC for each inner square.

Carry MC across back of work on inner squares, twisting yarn tog with CC at halfway point to catch MC.

Afghan
Bottom Border
With MC, cast on 162 sts.
Rows 1–4, 7–10: Put first st of row on holder, with MC knit to end of row.
Rows 5 and 6: Put first st of row on holder, with CC knit to end of row. (152 working sts plus 5 sts on holders at either end)
[Work Rows 1–28 of Checks pat] 11 times, work Rows 1–13.
Work Row 14, inc 1 st at end of row.

Top Border

Rows 1–4, 7–9: Put first st of row on holder. With MC, knit to end of row inc 1 st in last st.

Rows 5 and 6: Put first st of row on holder. With CC, knit to end of row inc 1 st in last st.

Row 10: Put first st of row on holder. With MC, bind off rem sts knitwise.

Side Borders

With RS facing using MC, pick up and knit 3 sts for every 4 rows along one side of afghan.

Remove first st of end border from holder and knit it.

Rows 1–4, 7–9: With MC, knit to last st of row, remove 1 st from holder and put on LH, sl last st of RH needle to LH needle, k2tog.

Rows 5 and 6: With CC knit to last st of row, remove 1 st from holder and put on LH, sl last st of RH needle to LH needle, k2tog.

Bind off knitwise with MC. ■

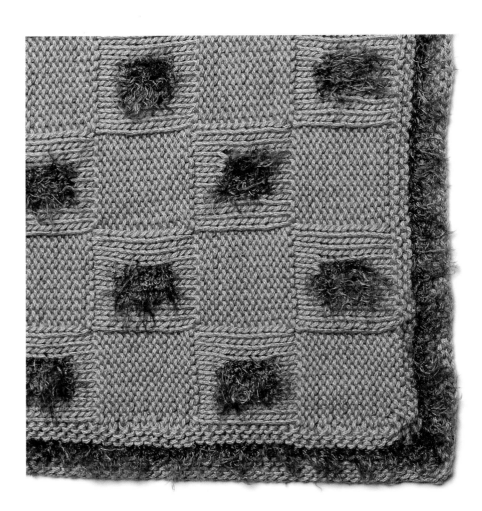

Simple Sensation

Design by LYNDA ROPER

BOLD BLACK AND WHITE SQUARES CREATE A DRAMATIC
LOOK IN A VERY MODERN AFGHAN.

Skill Level

 **EASY**

Finished Size
Approx 40 x 58 inches

Materials
- Plymouth Furlauro 100 percent nylon bulky weight eyelash yarn (82 yds/50g per ball): 3 balls white #1145 (A)
- Plymouth Sinsation 80 percent rayon/20 percnt wool bulky weight yarn (38 yds/50g per ball): 12 balls each black #3314 (B) and white #3300 (C)
- Size 10½ (6.5mm) 30-inch circular needle or size needed to obtain gauge

Gauge
10 sts and 16 rows = 4 inches/10cm in St st
To save time, take time to check gauge.

Pattern Notes
Circular needle is used to accommodate large number of sts. Do not join; work in rows. Use separate balls for each color section.
To avoid holes when changing colors, always bring new color up over old.

Afghan
With A, cast on 112 sts loosely.
Beg with knit row, work in St st for 8 rows.
Set up pat
Next row (RS): K8 A, [join B, k24, join C, k24] twice, join A, k8.
Work even in St st and established color pat for 35 more rows.
Keeping 8 sts at each end in A and reversing color block placement, work even for 36 more rows. (72 rows)
Work in established block pat until there is a total of 6 rows of blocks.
Change to A and work even in St st for 8 rows.
Bind off loosely. ■

Spiral Paths

Design by BARBARA VENISHNICK

LIGHT AND DARK SPIRAL OUTWARD IN CONTRASTING, EVER-INCREASING BLOCKS ON AN ULTRATHICK AFGHAN.

Skill Level
■ ■ ☐ ☐ **EASY**

Finished Size
Approx 56 x 56 inches

Materials
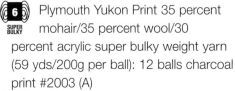 Plymouth Yukon Print 35 percent mohair/35 percent wool/30 percent acrylic super bulky weight yarn (59 yds/200g per ball): 12 balls charcoal print #2003 (A)

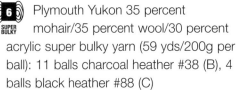 Plymouth Yukon 35 percent mohair/35 percent wool/30 percent acrylic super bulky yarn (59 yds/200g per ball): 11 balls charcoal heather #38 (B), 4 balls black heather #88 (C)

- Size 15 (10mm) 30-inch circular needle or size needed to obtain gauge

Gauge
9 sts and 18 rows = 4 inches/10cm in garter st
To save time, take time to check gauge.

Pattern Stitch
Garter Stitch
Every row: K1-tbl, knit to last st, sl 1 wyif.
Rep this row for pat.

Pattern Notes
Circular needle is used to accommodate large number of sts. Do not join; work in rows.
Refer to Fig. 1 for color placement and direction of work.

Afghan
Beg at center with A, cast on 10 sts.

Block 1
Work 20 rows [10 ridges] garter st pat.
With RS facing, bind off 9 sts.
Bind off last st with C.

Block 2
With C, pick up and knit 10 sts along left side of center square.
On this and all subsequent blocks, count last bound-off st of C as the first of these 10 sts.
Turn, work 1 row of garter st.
Change to B and work 18 rows of garter st pat.
Bind off 9 sts, bind off last st with C.

Block 3
With C, pick up and knit 10 sts along left side of Block 2, and 10 sts in cast-on edge of Block 1. (20 sts)
Turn, work 1 row of garter st.
Change to B and work 18 rows of garter st.
Bind off 19 sts, bind off last st with C.

Block 4
With C, pick up and knit 10 sts along left side of Block 3, and 10 sts along RS of Block 1. (20 sts)
Turn, work 1 row of garter st.
Change to A and work 18 rows of garter st.
Bind off 19 sts, bind off last st with C.

Block 5
With C, pick up and knit total of 30 sts

along left side of work.

Turn, work 1 row of garter st.

Change to B and work 18 rows of garter st.

Bind off 29 sts, bind off last st with C.

Block 6

With C, pick up and knit total of 30 sts along left side of work.

Turn, work 1 row of garter st.

Change to A and work 18 rows of garter st.

Bind off 29 sts, bind off last st with C.

Block 7

With C, pick up and knit 40 sts along left side of work.

Turn, work 1 row of garter st.

Change to A and work 18 rows of garter st.

Bind off 39 sts, bind off last st with C.

Block 8

With C, pick up and knit 40 sts along left side of work.

Turn, work 1 row of garter st.

Change to B and work 18 rows of garter st.

Bind off 39 sts, bind off last st with C.

Block 9

With C, pick up and knit 50 sts along left side of work.

Turn, work 1 row of garter st.

Change to A and work 18 rows of garter st.

Bind off 49 sts, bind off last st with C.

Block 10

With C, pick up and knit 50 sts along left side of work.

Turn, work 1 row of garter st.

Change to B and work 18 rows of garter st.

Bind off 49 sts, bind off last st with C.

Block 11

With C, pick up and knit 60 sts along left side of work.

Turn, work 1 row of garter st.

Change to B and work 18 rows of garter st.

Bind off 59 sts, bind off last st with C.

Block 12

With C, pick up and knit 60 sts along the left side of work.

Turn, work 1 row of garter st.

Change to A and work 18 rows of garter st.

Bind off 59 sts, bind off last st with C.

Block 13

With C, pick up and knit 70 sts along the left side of work.

Turn, work 1 row of garter st.

Change to B and work 18 rows of garter st.

Bind off 60 sts, bind off last st with C.

Block 14

With C, pick up and knit 70 sts along left side of work.

Turn, work 1 row of garter st.

Change to A and work 18 rows of garter st.

Bind off 69 sts, bind off last st with C.

Block 15

With C, pick up and knit 80 sts along the left side of work.

Turn, work 1 row of garter st.

Change to A and work 18 rows of garter st.

Bind off 79 sts, bind off last st with C.

Block 16

With C, pick up and knit 80 sts along the left side of work.

Turn, work 1 row of garter st.

Change to B and work 18 rows of garter st.

Bind off 79 sts, bind off last st with C.

Block 17

With C, pick up and knit 90 sts along left side of work.

Turn, work 1 row of garter st.

Change to A and work 18 rows of garter st.

Bind off 89 sts, bind off last st with C.

Block 18

With C, pick up and knit 90 sts along left side of work.

Turn, work 1 row of garter st.

Change to B and work 18 rows of garter st.
Bind off 89 sts, bind off last st with C

Block 19

With C, pick up and knit 100 sts along the
left side of work.
Turn, work 1 row of garter st.
Change to B and work 18 rows of garter st.
Bind off 99 sts, bind off last st with C.

Block 20

With C, pick up and knit 100 sts along the
left side of work.
Turn, work 1 row of garter st.
Change to A and work 18 rows of garter st.
Bind off 99 sts, bind off last st with C.

Block 21

With C, pick up and knit 110 sts along the
left side of work.
Turn, work 1 row of garter st.
Change to B and work 18 rows of garter st.
Bind off 109 sts, bind off last st with C.

Block 22

With C, pick up and knit 110 sts along the
left side of work.
Turn, work 1 row of garter st.
Change to A and work 18 rows of garter st.
Bind off 109 sts, bind off last st with C.

Block 23

With C, pick up and knit 120 sts along the
left side of work.
Turn, work 1 row of garter st.
Change to A and work 18 rows of garter st.
Bind off 119 sts, bind off last st with C.

Block 24

With C, pick up and knit 120 sts along the
left side of work.
Turn, work 1 row of garter st.
Change to B and work 18 rows of garter st.
Bind off 119 sts, bind off last st with C.

Outer Border

With C, pick up and knit 130 sts along
edge of Block 21 and end of Block 22.
Turn, knit 1 row on WS.
Turn, bind off all sts on the RS purlwise; **do
not** cut yarn.
Pick up and knit 119 sts along edge of
Block 22 and end of Block 23.
Turn, knit 1 row on WS.
Turn, bind off all sts on the RS purlwise; **do
not** cut yarn.
Work rem sides in same manner, picking
up 129 sts along 3rd side, and 119 sts on
final side. ■

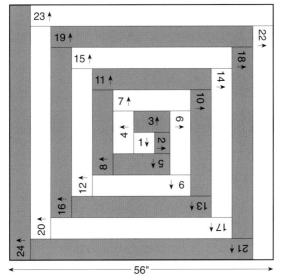

STITCH KEY	
☐	A
▨	B

56"

Fig. 1

Braided Cables Afghan

Design by GAYLE BUNN

OVERSIZED CABLES EXCHANGE COLOR PLACEMENT IN

THIS WARM AND HEFTY AFGHAN.

Skill Level

 INTERMEDIATE

Finished Size

Approx 45 x 56 inches (excluding fringe)

Materials

6 SUPER BULKY Plymouth Encore Mega 75 percent acrylic/25 percent wool super bulky weight yarn (64 yds/100g per skein): 13 skeins each stone #240 (MC) and charcoal heather #389 (CC)

- Size 15 (10mm) 36-inch circular needle or size needed to obtain gauge
- Cable needle
- Size M/13 (9mm) crochet hook

Gauge

10 sts and 12 rows = 4 inches/10cm in St st
To save time, take time to check gauge.

Pattern Notes

Circular needle is used to accommodate large number of sts. Do not join; work in rows.

Leave approx an 8-inch end of each color when casting on. This will be used later for fringe.

Entire afghan is worked in Intarsia method. Do not carry/strand yarn across back of work.

Use separate balls of yarn for each area of color.

To avoid holes when changing colors, always bring new color up over old.

Take extra care when working cables to ensure correct strand is in position when changing colors.

Special Abbreviations

C8B (Cable 8 Back): Sl 4 sts to cn and hold in back, k2 MC, k2 CC, (k2 MC, k2 CC) from cn.

C8F (Cable 8 Front): Sl 4 sts to cn and hold in front, k2 CC, k2 MC, (k2 CC, k2 MC) from cn.

Pattern Stitch

Braided Cables

Rows 1, 3, 7 and 9 (RS): *K2 CC, k2 MC; rep from * across.

Row 2 and all WS rows: K2 MC, *p2 CC, p2 MC; rep from * to last 2 sts, k2 CC.

Row 5: *K2 CC, C8B, k2 MC, C8F; rep from * to last 12 sts, k2 CC, C8B, k2 MC.

Row 10: Rep Row 2.

Rep Rows 1–10 for pat.

Afghan

[Cast on 2 sts with MC, cast on 2 sts with CC] 28 times. (112 sts)

Work even in Braided Cables pat until afghan measures approx 56 inches, ending with Row 8 of pat.

Bind off in pat, leaving an 8-inch end of each color.

Fringe

Cut strands of each color, each 16 inches long.

Fold each strand in half.

Working along cast-on edge, insert crochet hook from WS to RS next to existing fringe. Pull fold of fringe through fabric. Draw ends through lp and fasten tightly.

Rep along bound-off edge.

Trim fringe evenly. ■

Funky Flecks Throw

Design by SHEILA JONES

BRIGHT COLORS ALONG WITH THIS UNUSUAL
CARRY-ALONG YARN COMBINE FOR A UNIQUE
RETRO-LOOKING THROW.

Skill Level

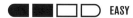 **EASY**

Finished Size
Approx 36 x 48 inches

Materials
- **3 LIGHT** Plymouth Wildflower D.K. 51 percent mercerized cotton/49 percent acrylic DK weight yarn (137 yds/50g per ball): 11 balls lime #58 (MC)
- Plymouth Collection Francaise Flirt 100 percent nylon DK weight yarn (93 yds/50g per ball): 19 balls rainbow #116 (CC)
- Size 7 (4.5mm) 32-inch circular needles or size needed to obtain gauge

Gauge
20 sts and 28 rows = 4 inches/10cm in St st
To save time, take time to check gauge.

Pattern Notes
One strand of each yarn is held tog throughout afghan.
Circular needle is used to accommodate large number of sts. Do not join; work in rows.

Throw
Cast on 180 sts.
Knit 3 rows.
Set up pat
Row 1 (RS) Knit.
Row 2: K3, purl to last 3 sts, k3.
Rep Rows 1 and 2 until throw measures 47½ inches, ending with Row 1 of pat.
Knit 3 rows.
Bind off knitwise on RS. ∎

Complementary Geometrics

Design by KENNITA TULLY

STRIPES AND SQUARES ARE BALANCED IN AN

ASYMMETRICAL REPEAT ON A MODERN-LOOKING THROW.

Skill Level
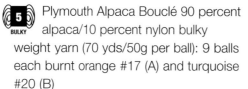 EASY

Finished Size
Approx 36 x 45 inches

Materials
 Plymouth Alpaca Bouclé 90 percent alpaca/10 percent nylon bulky weight yarn (70 yds/50g per ball): 9 balls each burnt orange #17 (A) and turquoise #20 (B)
• Size 11 (8mm) 30-inch circular needle or size needed to obtain gauge

Gauge
11 sts and 9 rows = 4 inches/10cm in garter st
To save time, take time to check gauge.

Pattern Stitches
Intarsia Blocks A
All RS rows: *K10 B, k10 A; rep from * across.
All WS rows: *K10 A, k10 B; rep from * across.

Intarsia Blocks B
All RS rows: *K10 A, k10 B; rep from * across.
All WS rows: *K10 B, k10 A; rep from * across.

Pattern Notes
Circular needle is used to accommodate large number of sts. Do not join; work in rows.
Throw is worked in garter st throughout. Wind separate balls or bobbins for each color area of intarsia blocks.
To avoid holes when changing colors, always bring new color up over old.

Throw
With A, cast on 100 sts.
Work even in following sequence:
[8 rows A, 8 rows B] 3 times.
16 rows Intarsia Blocks A, 16 rows Intarsia Blocks B.
8 rows each of A, B, A.
16 rows Intarsia blocks A.
8 rows each of B, A, B.
16 rows Intarsia Blocks A, 16 rows Intarsia Blocks B.
[8 rows A, 8 rows B] 3 times.
Bind off knitwise. ■

Park Avenue

Design by BARBARA VENISHNICK

ELEGANT WINDOWPANE SQUARES COMBINE WITH A
MOSAIC GOLD BORDER FOR A TRULY REFINED AFGHAN.

Skill Level

■■■□ **INTERMEDIATE**

Finished Size
Approx 45 x 52 inches

Materials
 Plymouth Baby Alpaca Grande 100 percent baby alpaca bulky weight yarn (110 yds/100g per hank): 14 hanks burgundy #2020 (MC)

 Plymouth 24K 82 percent nylon/18 percent lamé DK weight yarn (187 yds/50g per ball): 4 balls gold #1373 (CC)

• Size 9 (5.5mm) 39-inch circular needle or size needed to obtain gauge

Gauge
15 sts and 22 rows = 4 inches/10cm in St st with MC
To save time, take time to check gauge.

Special Abbrevation
M1 (Make 1): Make a backward lp and place on RH needle.

Pattern Stitch
Windowpane
Rows 1 (RS)–5: Knit.
Row 6: [K3, p11] 10 times, k3.
Rows 7, 9, 11, 13, 15, 17, 19 and 21: Knit.
Rows 8, 10, 12, 14, 16, 18, 20 and 22: Rep Row 6.
Rep Rows 1–22 for pat.

Pattern Notes
Circular needle is used to accommodate large number of sts. Do not join; work in rows.

Each row of chart is worked twice. Read RS rows from right to left; WS rows are read from left to right.

Pay close attention to Stitch and Color Key.
Knit 6 rows. Bind off all sts.

Afghan
With MC, cast on 163 sts.
Knit 1 row.
Work Rows 1–30 of Border chart.
Knit 4 rows MC.
Dec row (RS): K2, *ssk, k11, k2tog, k1; rep from * to last st, k1. (143 sts)
Beg with Row 7, work even in Windowpane pat until 12 squares have been completed.
Inc row (RS): *K3, M1, k11, M1; rep from * to last 3 sts, k3. (163 sts)
Knit 3 rows.
Work Rows 1–30 of Border chart.
With MC, bind off all sts.

Side Border
With MC and RS of work facing, pick up and knit 17 sts along short edge of bottom border, 16 sts along each windowpane, 18 sts along short edge of top border. (227 sts)
Knit 1 row.
Work Rows 1–30 of Border chart.
With MC, knit 3 rows.
Bind off knitwise on WS.
Rep for opposite side.

End Trim

With MC and RS facing, pick up and knit 15 sts along short end of side border, 1 st in each cast-on st, and 15 sts along short end of rem side border.
Knit 2 rows.
Bind off knitwise on WS.
Rep along bound-off edge. ■

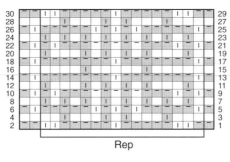

Rep

PARK AVENUE BORDER CHART

COLOR &STITCH KEY
- ☐ MC
- ▨ CC
- ☐ K on RS, p on WS
- − K on RS and WS
- ˡ Sl 1 wyib on RS, sl 1 wyif on WS

Easy Mosaic Afghan

Design by MELISSA LEAPMAN

THE SOFT LUXURY OF BABY ALPACA WILL ENVELOPE
YOU ON A CHILLY EVENING. GIVE IT A PLACE OF HONOR
NEXT TO THE FIREPLACE.

Skill Level
◼◼◻◻ EASY

Finished Size
Approx 53 x 62 inches (excluding fringe)

Materials
 Plymouth Baby Alpaca Grande 100
percent baby alpaca bulky weight
yarn (110 yds/100g per hank): 10 hanks
each putty #202 (A) and hunter green
#679 (B)
• Size 10½ (6.5mm) 30-inch circular needle
or size needed to obtain gauge

Gauge
16 sts and 32 rows = 4 inches/10cm in
pat st
To save time, take time to check gauge.

Pattern Notes
Circular needle is used to accommodate
large number of sts. Do not join; work
in rows.
Slip all sts purlwise.

Afghan
With A, cast on 211 sts.
Row 1 (RS): With A, knit.
Row 2: With A, knit.
Row 3: With B, k5, *sl 1 wyib, k7; rep from
*, end last rep sl 1 wyib, k5.

Row 4: With B, k5, *sl 1 wyif, k7; rep from
*, end last rep sl 1 wyif, k5.
Row 5: With A, [k1, sl 1 wyib] twice, *k3, [sl
1 wyib, k1] twice, sl 1 wyib; rep from *, end
last rep k3, [sl 1 wyib, k1] twice.
Row 6: With A, [k1, sl 1 wyif] twice, *k3, [sl
1 wyif, k1] twice, sl 1 wyif; rep from *, end
last rep k3, [sl 1 wyif, k1] twice.
Row 7: With B, k4, *sl 1 wyib, k1, sl 1 wyib,
k5; rep from *, end last rep sl 1 wyib, k1, sl
1 wyib, k4.
Row 8: With B, k4, *sl 1 wyif, k1, sl 1 wyif,
k5; rep from *, end last rep sl 1 wyif, k1, sl
1 wyif, k4.
Row 9: With A, k2, *[sl 1 wyib, k2] twice, sl
1 wyib, k1; rep from *, end last rep k1.
Row 10: With A, k2, *[sl 1 wyif, k2] twice, sl
1 wyif, k1; rep from *, end last rep k1.
Row 11: With B, *k3, sl 1 wyib; rep from *,
end last rep k3.
Row 12: With B, *k3, sl 1 wyif; rep from *,
end last rep k3.
Row 13: With A, k2, *sl 1 wyib, k1; rep
from *, end last rep k1.
Row 14: With A, k2, *sl 1 wyif, k1; rep from
*, end last rep k1.
Rows 15 and 16: With B, rep Rows 11
and 12.
Rows 17 and 18: With A, rep Rows 9
and 10.
Rows 19 and 20: With B, rep Rows 7
and 8.

Rows 21 and 22: With A, rep Rows 5 and 6.

Rows 23 and 24: With B, rep Rows 3 and 4.

Rep Rows 1–24 until afghan measures approx 62 inches, ending with Row 2 of pat.

Bind off.

Fringe

Cut strands of yarn, each 14 inches long.

Holding 5 strands tog and mixing colors as desired, fold each group in half.

Working along cast-on edge, insert crochet hook from WS to RS.

Pull fold of fringe through fabric. Draw ends through lp and fasten tightly.

Fringe is worked in every 7th st.

Rep along bound-off edge.

Trim fringe evenly. ■

Funky Foursome

Design by NAZANIN FARD

FOUR YARNS IN VARYING TEXTURES COMBINE IN A CHEVRON-STRIPE PATTERN IN THIS SUMPTUOUS AFGHAN. TASSELS DECORATE THE POINTS OF EACH CHEVRON.

Skill Level
 **EASY**

Finished Size
Approx 40 x 53 inches (excluding tassels)

Materials
 Plymouth Rimini Rainbow 60 percent acrylic/40 percent wool super bulky yarn (38 yds/50g per ball): 6 balls orange sunset #19 (A)

 Plymouth 24K 82 percent nylon/18 percent lamé worsted weight yarn (187 yds/50g per ball): 3 balls rust sparkle #1356 (B)

 Plymouth Alpaca Bouclé 90 percent alpaca/10 percent nylon super bulky yarn (70 yds/50g per ball): 8 balls burnt orange #17 (C)

 Plymouth Spazzini 75 percent wool/25 percent nylon bulky weight yarn (72 yds/50g per ball): 9 balls autumn leaves #936 (D)

- Size 15 (10mm) 30-inch circular needle or size needed to obtain gauge
- Size J/10 (6mm) crochet hook
- 6-inch piece of cardboard

Gauge
8 sts and 18 rows (9 ridges) = 4 inches/10cm in pat st
To save time, take time to check gauge.

Special Abbreviation
M1 (Make 1): Make a backward lp and place on RH needle.

Pattern Stitches
A. Ridges
Row 1 (WS): Knit.
Row 2: *K1, M1, k8, ssk, k1, k2tog, k8, M1; rep from * to last st, k1.
Rep Rows 1–2 for pat.

B. Color Stripe Sequence
Work 2 rows each of A, 3 strands B held tog, 2 strands C held tog, 3 strands D held tog.

Pattern Notes
Circular needle is used to accommodate large number of sts. Do not join; work in rows.

Afghan
With A, cast on 112 sts.
Work even in Color Stripe sequence until 17 reps (68 ridges) have been completed.
Knit 2 rows A.
Bind off loosely.

Side Edging
With C, work 1 row of sc along side edge of afghan.
Rep for other side.

Tassel
Make 11
Cut 2 strands of B, each about 8 inches long and set aside.

Holding 1 strand of each yarn tog, wrap yarn around cardboard 4 times.

Using 1 reserved strand, tie one end; cut opposite end.

Wrap 2nd strand around tassel, about 1 inch below fold.

Tie tightly and hide ends in tassel.

Trim ends even.

Attach 1 tassel to each point of afghan. ■

Monet Miters Throw

Design by DIANE ZANGL

SOFT MOHAIR COMBINES WITH GLITZ IN AN INTERESTING TWIST ON SHAPE AND COLOR. THE MITERED SQUARES ARE KNIT IN GARTER STITCH AND JOINED AS THEY ARE WORKED. GARTER BANDS SEPARATE THE ROWS OF BLOCKS.

Skill Level

 INTERMEDIATE

Finished Size

Approx 44 x 56 inches

Materials

- **(4 MEDIUM)** Plymouth Le Fibre Nobili Imperiale 80 percent mohair/20 percent nylon worsted weight yarn (110 yds/25g per ball): 10 balls each olive #4122 (A) and taupe #4121 (B); 7 balls off-white #4102 (C)
- **(5 BULKY)** Plymouth Odyssey Glitz 60 percent nylon/37 percent wool/3 percent lamé bulky weight novelty yarn (65 yds/ 50g per ball): 21 balls spring #900 (CC)
- Size 11 (8mm) 36-inch circular and 2 (10-inch) double pointed needles

Gauge

10 sts and 20 rows = 4 inches/10cm in garter st
To save time, take time to check gauge.

Special Techniques & Abbreviations

Cable Cast On: *Insert RH needle between last 2 sts on LH needle, wrap yarn around needle as if to knit and pull through to make a new st, place new st on LH needle; rep from * as directed.

CDD (Centered Double Decrease): Sl 2 sts as if to k2tog, k1, pass 2 sl sts over knit st. Center st will lie on top.

Pattern Stitch

Basic Square

Row 1 (WS): Knit to marked st, p1, knit to end of row.

Row 2: Knit to 1 st before marked st, CDD, knit to end of row.

Rep Rows 1 and 2 until 1 st rem. Leave last st on needle, cut mohair only. Join next color.

Pattern Notes

Two dpns are used for squares; circular needle is used for dividing bands and outer borders.

One strand of glitz and 2 strands of mohair (either A, B or C) are held tog throughout throw. Colors are referred to by the mohair letter only.

When changing colors, cut mohair only. Glitz is carried through entire throw.

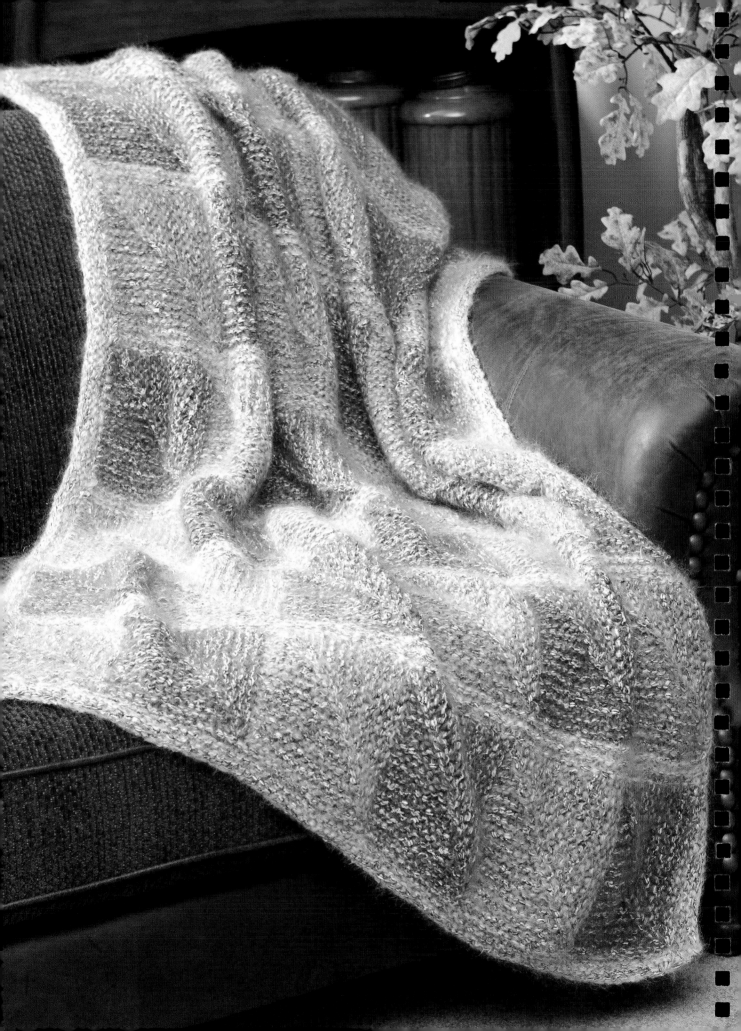

Throw

With dpn, using 2 strands of A and 1 strand of CC held tog, Cable Cast On 33 sts. Mark center st.

Work Basic Square, change to B.

Pick up and knit 16 sts (1 st in each ridge) along left edge of square just worked, mark last st, Cable Cast On 16 sts. (33 sts)

Work Basic Square, change to A.

Continue alternating squares of A and B until there are 6 squares in the row. Fasten off last st.

*Dividing Band

With circular needle and RS facing, using 2 strands of C and 1 strand of CC held tog, pick up and knit 16 sts along top edge of each square. (96 sts)

Knit 5 rows.

Cut C; leave sts on needle.

Second Row of Squares

With B and dpn, cable cast on 17 sts, mark last st, knit across 16 sts of dividing band, turn. (33 sts on dpn, remainder left on circular needle)

Work Basic Square, leaving last st on needle. Change to A.

Continue adding squares in alternating colors by picking up and knitting 16 sts along square just completed and knitting another 16 sts along top of dividing band. (33 sts when beg each square)

Rep from *, until there are 7 rows of squares with a dividing band between each row.

Rep dividing band.

Bind off loosely.

End Border

With 2 strands of C and 1 strand of CC held tog, pick up and knit 96 sts along beg end of throw.

Knit 5 rows.

Bind off loosely.

Side Border

Work as for end border, picking up and knitting 16 sts in each square and 3 sts in each dividing band. (136 sts)

Knit 5 rows.

Bind off loosely.

Rep for 2nd side. ■

Rainbow Fiesta

Design by BONNIE FRANZ

THIS COZY AFGHAN IS EASY ENOUGH FOR THE NEWEST KNITTER!

Skill Level

 BEGINNER

Finished Size
Approx 49 x 60 inches

Materials
- **6 SUPER BULKY** Plymouth Rimini Rainbow 60 percent acrylic/40 percent wool super bulky weight yarn (38 yds/50g per ball): 13 balls fiesta #19
- Size 15 (10mm) 24-inch circular needle or size needed to obtain gauge

Gauge
5 sts and 9 rows = 4 inches/10cm in pat
To save time, take time to check gauge.

Afghan
Cast on 59 sts.

Work even in St st until afghan measures 60 inches, ending with a WS row.

Drop st bind-off row: *Bind off 4 sts, drop next st from LH needle and allow it to unravel to cast-on row, forming a long runner, [cast on 1 st and immediately bind it off] 3 times; rep from * to last 4 sts, bind off 4 sts. ∎

Walkabout Throw

Design by MELISSA LEAPMAN

DESERT COLORS ARE REMINISCENT OF THE
AUSTRALIAN OUTBACK IN THIS EFFORTLESS
FRINGED THROW.

Skill Level
 EASY

Finished Size
Approx 46 x 54 inches (excluding fringe)

Materials
 Plymouth Outback Wool 100
percent virgin wool worsted weight
yarn (370 yds/200g per skein): 5 skeins
Southwest print #995
- Size 8 (5mm) 36-inch circular needle or
  size needed to obtain gauge
- Size I/9 (5.5mm) crochet hook

Gauge
18 sts and 26 rows = 4 inches/10cm in
Walkabout pat
To save time, take time to check gauge.

Pattern Stitch
Walkabout (multiple of 7 sts + 4)
Row 1 (RS): K4, *yo, sl next st purlwise,
k2tog, psso, yo, k4; rep from * across row.
Rows 2 and 3: Knit.
Row 4: Purl.
Rep Rows 1–4 for pat.

Pattern Note
Circular needle is used to accommodate
large number of sts. Do not join; work
in rows.

Throw
Cast on 207 sts.
Work even in Walkabout pat until throw
measures approx 54 inches, ending with
Row 2 of pat.
Bind off knitwise.

Fringe
Cut strands of yarn, each 12 inches long.
Holding 7 strands tog, fold each group
in half.
Working along cast-on edge, insert crochet
hook from WS to RS of k4 section. Pull fold
of fringe through fabric. Draw ends through
lp and fasten tightly.
Rep fringe in each k4 section.
Rep along bound-off edge.
Trim fringe evenly. ■

Royal Luxury

Design by BONNIE FRANZ

THIS RICHLY COLORED, LUXURIOUSLY COZY AFGHAN IS
SURPRISINGLY EASY TO MAKE.

Skill Level
■□□□ BEGINNER

Finished Size
Approx 45 x 55 inches

Materials
 Plymouth Alpaca Bouclé 90 percent
alpaca/10 percent nylon super bulky
weight yarn (70 yds/50g per ball): 18
balls royal red #18
- Size 10½ (6.5mm) 30-inch circular
  needle or size needed to obtain gauge

Gauge
12 sts and 20 rows = 4 inches/10cm in
Openwork pat
To save time, take time to check gauge.

Pattern Stitch
Openwork
Rows 1 (RS)–4: Knit.
Row 5: *K2tog, yo; rep from * to last st, k1.
Rows 6–9: Knit.
Rows 10, 12, 14 and 16: Purl.
Rows 11, 13 and 15: Knit.
Rep Rows 1–16 for pat.

Pattern Note
Circular needles are used to accommodate
large number of sts. Do not join; work
in rows.

Afghan
Cast on 135 sts.
Work even in Openwork pat until afghan
measures approx 55 inches, ending with
Row 8 of pat.
Bind off knitwise on RS. ■

Cherries Summer

Design by LILLIANE DICKINSON

SCRUMPTIOUS CHERRIES EMBELLISH A COLORFUL
SUMMER AFGHAN. USE IT TO ADD A CHEERFUL TOUCH
TO A SCREENED-IN PORCH.

Skill Level

 **INTERMEDIATE**

Finished Size

Approx 47 x 68 inches

Materials

4 MEDIUM Plymouth Fantasy Naturale 100
percent mercerized cotton worsted
weight yarn (140 yds/100g per skein): 2
skeins yellow #1242 (A); 4 skeins cherry
red #3611 (B); 3 skeins each white
#8001 (C), gold #1404 (D) and blue
#2574 (F); 1 skein lime green #8019 (E)

- Size 7 (4.5mm) straight needles
- Size 8 (5mm) 36-inch circular needle or
  size needed to obtain gauge
- Stitch markers

Gauge

17 sts and 20 rows = 4 inches/10cm in St
st with larger needles
To save time, take time to check gauge.

Pattern Notes

Circular needle is used to accommodate
large number of sts. Do not join; work
in rows.
Color pat is worked in stranded method
from charts.
Afghan is outlined with a short garter st
edging, which is worked directly
onto the piece. A scallop border is
worked separately and sewn to afghan
upon completion.

Afghan

With larger needle and E, cast on 176 sts.
Knit 1 row. Change to A.
*Beg with a RS row, work in St st for 10
rows.
Refer to Chart A, [work rep] 17 times; rep
first 6 sts.
Change to D, work in St st for 6 rows.
Refer to Chart B, [work rep] 8 times, pm
between each rep.
Change to D, work in St st for 6 rows
Change to A, work in St st for 10 rows
Refer to Chart C, [work rep] 16 times.
Change to D, work in St st for 6 rows.
Rep from * twice.
Change to E and knit 2 rows.
Bind off all sts.

Side Edging

With RS facing and using larger needle and
E, pick up and knit 3 sts for every 4 rows
along 1 side edge.
Knit 1 row
Bind off.
Rep along rem side edge.

Scallop Border

With smaller needles and B, cast on 5 sts.
Row 1: Knit.
Row 2: Knit to last 2 sts, knit in front and
back of next st, k1. (6 sts)
Row 3: K1, knit in front and back of next
st, knit to end. (7 sts)
Rows 4–9: Rep Rows 2 and 3 until there
are 13 sts on needle.
Row 10: Knit.

Row 11: K1, k2tog, knit to end. (12 sts)

Row 12: Knit to last 3 sts, k2tog, k1. (11 sts)

Rows 13–18: Rep Rows 11 and 12 until 5 sts rem.

[Rep Rows 1–18] 73 times.

Bind off.

Assembly

With B, sew border to afghan, having 22 points along each long side and 15 at both top and bottom edges.

Border should fit neatly around afghan when slightly stretched at the straight edges, but should lie flat at the corners. Sew cast-on and bound-off edges of border tog. ■

COLOR KEY
☐ Yellow (A)
■ Cherry red (B)
☐ White (C)
☐ Gold (D)
■ Lime green (E)
■ Blue (F)

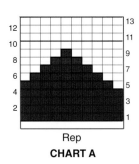

Rep

CHART A

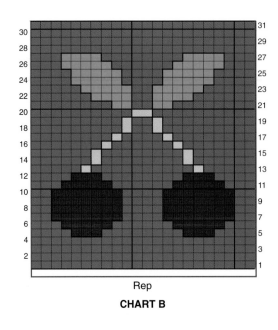

Rep

CHART B

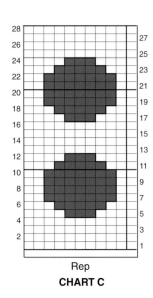

Rep

CHART C

Braided Leaf Sophisticate

Design by KATHARINE HUNT

A CLASSIC AFGHAN WORKED IN PANELS AND JOINED IS ALWAYS A WELCOME GIFT FOR ANY OCCASION.

Skill Level

 INTERMEDIATE

Finished Size

Approx 48 x 60 inches

Materials

Plymouth Encore Worsted 75 percent acrylic/25 percent wool worsted weight yarn (200 yds/100g per ball): 9 balls light putty #1202 (A), 4 balls medium putty #1203 (B)
- Size 7 (4.5mm) needles or size needed to obtain gauge
- Cable needle

Gauge

Braided Leaf Panel = 9½ inches, lightly blocked
Cable Panel = 4 inches, lightly blocked
To save time, take time to check gauge.

Special Abbreviations

C3F (Cross 3 Front): Sl 2 sts to cn and hold in front, k1, k2 from cn.

C3B (Cross 3 Back): Sl 1 st to cn and hold in back, k2, k1 from cn.

T3F (Twist 3 Front): Sl 2 sts to cn and hold in front, p1, k2 from cn.

T3B (Twist 3 Back): Sl 1 st to cn and hold in back, k2, p1 from cn.

T5R (Twist 5 Right): Sl 3 sts to cn and hold in back, k2, (p1, k2) from cn.

Afghan

Braided Leaf Panel
Make 4

With A cast on 41 sts.
Knit 6 rows.

Row 1 (RS): K3, yo, k2tog, k2, k2tog, [yo, k2tog] 3 times, yo, k1, yo, k2, k2tog, k4, k2tog, k2, [yo, k2tog] 3 times, yo, k3, yo, k2tog, k2.

Row 2: K7, p26, k8.

Row 3: K3, yo, k2tog, k1, k2tog, [yo, k2tog] 3 times, yo, k3, yo, [k2, k2tog] twice, k2, [yo, k2tog] 3 times, yo, k4, yo, k2tog, k2.

Row 4: K8, p26, k7.

Row 5: K3, yo, [k2tog] twice, [yo, k2tog] 3 times, yo, k5, yo, k2, [k2tog] twice, k2, [yo, k2tog] 3 times, yo, k5, yo, k2tog, k2.

Row 6: K9, p26, k6.

Row 7: K3, yo, k2tog, k2, [yo, ssk] 3 times, yo, k2, k2tog, k4, k2tog, k2, yo, k1, [yo, ssk] 4 times, k3, yo, k2tog, k2.

Row 8: Rep Row 4.

Row 9: K3, yo, k2tog, k3, [yo, ssk] 3 times, yo, k2, [k2tog, k2] twice, yo, k3, [yo, ssk] 4 times, k2, yo, k2tog, k2.

Row 10: Rep Row 2.

Row 11: K3, yo, k2tog, k4, [yo, ssk] 3 times, yo, k2, [k2tog] twice, k2, yo, k5, [yo, ssk] 4 times, k1, yo, k2tog, k2.

Row 12: K6, p26, k9.

Rep Rows 1–12 for a total of 39 reps, or until panel measures approx 60 inches ending with Row 12.

Knit 7 Rows.

Bind off knitwise on WS.

Cable Panel
Make 3

With B, cast on 23 sts.

Knit 6 rows.

Row 1 (RS): K3, yo, k2tog, k4, p5, k5, yo, k2tog, k2.

Row 2: K7, p2, k5, p2, k7.

Row 3: K3, yo, k2tog, k2, C3F, p3, C3B, k3, yo, k2tog, k2.

Row 4: K8, p2, k3, p2, k8.

Row 5: K3, yo, k2tog, k3, C3F, p1, C3B, k4, yo, k2tog, k2.

Row 6: K9, p2, k1, p2, k9.

Row 7: K3, yo, k2tog, k4, T5R, k5, yo, k2tog, k2.

Row 8: Rep Row 6.

Row 9: K3, yo, k2tog, k3, T3B, p1, T3F, k4, yo, k2tog, k2.

Row 10: Rep Row 4.

Row 11: K3, yo, k2tog, k2, T3B, p3, T3F, k3, yo, k2tog, k2.

Row 12: Rep Row 2.

Rep Rows 1–12 for a total of 39 reps, or until panel measures approx 60 inches ending with Row 12.

Knit 7 Rows.

Bind off knitwise on WS.

Assembly

On a clean, dry surface, pin panels to size. Cover with damp cloth and leave overnight to dry.

Alternating widths, sew panels tog as follows, beg and ending with a Braided Leaf panel.

Referring to Fig. 1, insert needle (from below) under **bottom lp** of garter st on one side of seam and then under **top lp** of a corresponding st on the opposite side. **Do not skip any sts.**

Continue alternating from side to side, pulling yarn in direction of seam, thus causing lps from each side to merge and form a continuous row of garter st bumps. ■

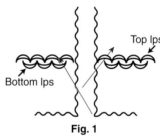

Fig. 1
Sewing Panels
Braided Leaf Sophisticate

Guernsey Tweed Afghan

Design by GAYLE BUNN

CLASSIC FISHERMAN PATTERNS AND SEASCAPE

COLORS ARE FEATURED IN THIS AFGHAN. THE SUBTLE,

STRIPED BORDERS ARE WORKED LAST.

Skill Level

■■■□ INTERMEDIATE

Finished Size

Approx 48 x 59 inches

Materials

4 MEDIUM Plymouth Encore Worsted Heather 75 percent acrylic/25 percent wool worsted weight yarn (200 yds/100g per ball): 21 balls dark blue/green tweed #670 (MC), 5 balls light blue/green tweed #678 (CC)

- Size 10½ (6.5mm) 30-inch circular needle or size needed to obtain gauge
- Cable needle

Gauge

14 sts and 21 rows = 4 inches/10cm in St st with 2 strands of yarn held tog
To save time, take time to check gauge.

Pattern Stitch

Border Stripe Sequence

Work 2 rows MC, then *4 rows each of MC and CC held tog, CC only, MC and CC held tog, MC only. Rep from * once.

Pattern Notes

Circular needle is used to accommodate large number of sts. Do not join; work in rows.

Two strands of yarn are held tog for entire afghan.

Afghan

With 2 strands of MC held tog, cast on 140 sts loosely.

Set up pat

Next row (RS): [P1, k1] twice, work Row 1 of Chart A, [work Row 1 of Chart B, work Row 1 of Chart A] 6 times [k1, p1] twice.

Row 2: [P1, k1] twice, work Row 2 of Chart A, [work Row 2 of Chart B, work Row 2 of Chart A] 6 times [k1, p1] twice.

Keeping first and last 4 sts in established Seed pat, and working rem sts from charts, work even until afghan measures approx 45 inches, ending with Row 12 of Chart B.

Top Border

Dec row (RS): *K3, k2tog, k4, k2tog; rep from * to last 8 sts, k3, k2tog, k3. (115 sts)

Row 2: P1, *k1, p1; rep from * across. This sets up Seed pat.

Working in established Seed pat and Border Stripe sequence, inc 1 st each end

of every RS row, working added sts into pat. (149 sts)
Bind off in pat.

Bottom Border

With RS facing and 2 strands of MC, pick up and knit 115 sts evenly across cast-on edge.
Beg with Row 2, work as for top border.

Side Border

With RS facing and 2 strands of MC, pick up and knit 149 sts along 1 side edge.
Beg with Row 2, work as for top border. (183 sts)
Rep for opposite side.

Finishing

Sew mitered corners of borders tog. ■

STITCH KEY
☐ K on RS, p on WS
⊟ P on RS, k on WS
▱ Sl 3 sts to cn and hold in front, k3, k3 from cn.

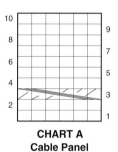

CHART A
Cable Panel

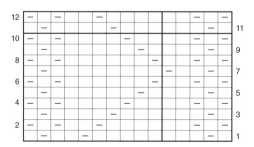

CHART B
Zigzag Panel

Smocking Stripes

Design by KATHARINE HUNT

SIMPLE STRIPES ARE CHANGED INTO SMOCKING WITH
THE ADDITION OF A FEW EMBROIDERY STITCHES.

Skill Level
 **EASY**

Finished Size
Approx 44 x 52 inches

Materials
Plymouth Fantasy Naturale 100
percent mercerized cotton worsted
weight yarn (140 yds/100g per skein): 8
skeins salmon #4548 (MC), 5 skeins light
kiwi #8011 (A), 3 skeins ecru #8176 (B)
- Size 8 (5mm) 29-inch circular needle or
size needed to obtain gauge
- Tapestry needle
- Size H/8 (5mm) crochet hook (optional)
- Split-ring or coilless stitch markers

Gauge
17 sts and 21 rows = 4 inches/10cm in St
st, lightly blocked
To save time, take time to check gauge.

Pattern Stitch
Shells
Rows 1 (RS)–4: Knit.
Row 5: K4, [yo twice, k1] 3 times, yo twice,
k2. (17 sts)
Row 6: K3, [p1, knit in front and back of
double yo] 3 times, p1, k4.
Rows 7– 9: Knit.
Row 10: K11, wrapping yarn twice around
needle for each st, yo twice, k6. (19 sts)
Row 11: K6, (p1, k1) into next st, sl next
11 sts to RH needle dropping extra lps,

return sts to LH needle and knit these 11
sts tog. (9 sts)
Row 12: Knit, pulling first st tightly.
Rep Rows 1–12 for pat.

Pattern Notes
Circular needle is used to accommodate
large number of sts. Do not join; work
in rows.
Carry CC along edge of work, twisting
over MC on RS rows. Do not cut CC
between stripes
For shell border, knit in front then in back of
double yo on following row.
Use crochet hook if you find it is difficult to
pull the st through when knitting 11 sts tog.
If extra length (less than a full shell) is
needed to match length of afghan, work a
few extra rows in garter st.

Afghan
With MC, cast on 175 sts.
Knit 2 rows, marking Row 1 as RS
*With MC work 16 rows in St st.
With B knit 2 rows, purl 1 row, knit 1 row.
[With MC work in St st for 4 rows. With B
knit 2 rows, purl 1 row, knit 1 row] 3 times.*
Repeat from * to * using A instead of B.
Continue in this manner until 7 sets of
contrast ribs are complete, ending with a
set of B.
With MC work in St st for 15 rows.
Knit 2 rows.
Bind off knitwise on WS.
Block on a clean, dry surface by pinning

afghan to size and covering with damp cloth. Leave overnight to dry.

Smocking

On first and 2nd contrast stripe, count 15 sts from edge, mark 16th st. This is the st to be smocked.

Continue across, marking every 16th st of both rows, ending with 15 sts.

Referring to photo, with tapestry needle and matching color, sew contrast stripe 1 to stripe 2 at each marked st, taking in full height of the ribs.

On reverse side, tie off smocking strand tightly and trim ends.

Shift the smocking on stripes 2 and 3 so 8th st is first st marked, mark each following 16th st, ending with 7 sts.

Revert to original spacing on stripes 3 and 4.

Continue in this manner until smocking on all sets of stripes is complete.

Side Border

With RS facing and A, pick up and knit 155 sts along 1 side of afghan from top to bottom.

Work in garter st for 6 rows.

Bind off knitwise on WS.

Rep for opposite side.

Shell Borders
Make 2

With A, cast on 9 stitches.

Knit 2 rows.

Work even in Shells pat until length matches short end of afghan.

Sew 1 border to each short end of afghan, taking care to align garter st rows at ends of border with garter sts on side edgings.

Push each shell from the back so it is fully rounded and puffed. ■

Reversible Diamonds

Design by SHARI HAUX

TWO FOR THE PRICE OF ONE! THE DIAMOND PATTERN HAS A DIFFERENT TEXTURE ON EITHER SIDE.

Skill Level
 INTERMEDIATE

Finished Size
Approx 57 x 51 inches

Materials
- Plymouth Encore Worsted 75 percent acrylic/25 percent wool worsted weight yarn (200 yds/100g per ball): 8 balls medium sage #1232
- Size 10 (6mm) 30-inch circular needle or size needed to obtain gauge
- Stitch markers

Gauge
16 sts and 20 rows = 4 inches/10cm in Diamonds pat
To save time, take time to check gauge.

Pattern Stitches
A. Seed Border
Row 1 (RS): K1, *p1, k1; rep from * across.
Rows 2 and 4: K1, purl to last st, k1.
Row 3: K2, *p1, k1; rep from * to last st, k1.
Rep Rows 1–4 for pat.

B. Diamonds
Row 1 (RS): K4, p5, *k7, p5; rep from * to last 4 sts, k4.
Row 2 and all WS rows: Knit or purl the sts as they present themselves.
Row 3: K3, p3, k1, p3, *k5, p3, k1, p3; rep from * to last 3 sts, k3.
Row 5: K2, p3, *k3, p3; rep from * to last 2 sts, k2.

Row 7: K1, *p3, k5, p3, k1; rep from * across.
Row 9: P3, k7, *p5, k7; rep from * to last 3 sts, p3.
Row 11: P2, k9, *p3, k9; rep from * to last 2 sts, p2.
Row 13: Rep Row 9.
Row 15: Rep Row 7.
Row 17: Rep Row 5.
Row 19: Rep Row 3.
Row 21: Rep Row 1.
Row 23: K5, p3, *k9, p3; rep from * to last 5 sts, k5.
Row 24: P5, k3, *p9, k3; rep from * to last 5 sts, p5.
Rep Rows 1–24 for pat.

Pattern Note
Circular needle is used to accommodate large number of sts. Do not join; work in rows.

Afghan
Cast on 195 sts.
Work even in Seed Border pat for 12 rows.
Set up pat
Next row (RS): Work Seed Border over 13 sts, pm, work Diamonds pat to last 13 sts, pm, Seed Border over 13 sts.
Work even in established pat until afghan measures approx 53 inches, ending with Row 12 of Diamonds pat.
Remove markers and work 12 rows of Seed Border pat.
Bind off in pat. ■

Summer Sunshine

Design by SHEILA JONES

INTARSIA BORDERS ADD A TOUCH OF SOFTNESS TO THIS BULKY AFGHAN.

Skill Level

 **INTERMEDIATE**

Finished Size
Approx 48 x 60 inches

Materials
 Plymouth Fantasy Naturale 100 mercerized cotton worsted weight yarn (140 yds/100g per skein): 26 skeins sunshine #1404 (MC)
- Plymouth Firenze 40 percent nylon/30 percent wool/30 percent acrylic bulky weight eyelash yarn (50g/55 yds per ball): 4 balls bronze #451 (CC)
- Size 11 (8mm) 40-inch circular needle or size needed to obtain gauge

Gauge
14 sts and 21 rows = 4 inches/10cm in pat st
To save time, take time to check gauge.

Pattern Notes
Circular needle is used to accommodate large number of sts. Do not join; work in rows.
Intarsia method is used when working side borders.
To avoid holes when changing colors, always bring new color up over old.
Two strands of yarn are held tog for entire afghan.

Afghan
With 2 strands of CC held tog, cast on 163 sts.
Knit 1 row.
Next row: K1 CC, with 2 strands MC held tog knit to last st, join 2nd ball of CC, k1.
[Rep last row] 3 times.
Beg pat
Rows 1 and 3 (RS): K1 CC, *with MC k2, sl 1k wyib; rep from * to last 3 sts, k2 MC, k1 CC.
Rows 2 and 4: K1 CC, *with MC k1, p1, *sl 1p wyif, p2; rep from * to last 4 sts, sl 1p wyif, p1, k1 MC, k1 CC.
Row 5: K1CC, with MC, knit to last st being careful not to twist sl sts, k1 CC.
Row 6: K1 CC, with MC, purl to last st, k1 CC
Work even in established pat until afghan measures approx 59 inches, ending with Row 5.
Next row: K1 CC, with MC, knit to last st, k1 CC.
[Rep last row] twice.
Cut MC; with CC, bind off knitwise on RS. ■

Pool Reflections

Design by Melissa Leapman

THIS SUMMER THROW COMBINES REFRESHING COLOR WITH GENTLE OPENWORK IN AN EASILY REMEMBERED PATTERN.

Skill Level

 EASY

Finished Size

Approx 45 x 60 inches

Materials

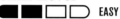 Plymouth Fantasy Naturale 100 percent mercerized cotton (140 yds/100g per hank): 14 hanks pool #8012
- Size 7 (4.5mm) 30-inch circular needle
- Size 8 (5mm) 30-inch circular needle or size needed to obtain gauge

Gauge

16 sts and 24 rows = 4 inches/10cm in pat st with larger needles
To save time, take time to check gauge.

Pattern Stitch

Eyelets

Row 1 (RS): Knit.
Row 2: Purl.
Row 3: K2, *yo, k2tog; rep from * to last st, k1.
Row 4: Purl.
Rows 5 and 6: Knit.
Rows 7 and 8: Rep Rows 1 and 2.
Row 9: K3, *yo, ssk; rep from * to last 2 sts, k2.
Row 10: Purl.
Rows 11 and 12: Rep Rows 5 and 6.
Rep Rows 1–12 for pat.

Pattern Note

Circular needle is used to accommodate large number of sts. Do not join; work in rows.

Throw

With smaller needle, cast on 181 sts. Work in garter st for 8 rows. Change to larger needle.
Work even in Eyelet pat until throw measures approx 59 inches, ending with Row 6 or 12 of pat.
Change to smaller needle.
Work even in garter st for 8 rows.
Bind off loosely. ∎

Climbing Roses

Design by SHARI HAUX

A SOFT COLOR AND PETITE CABLES EMBELLISH A TIMELESS AFGHAN. PICOT-HEMMED BORDERS ADD A ROMANTIC TOUCH.

Skill Level
 EASY

Finished Size
Approx 52 x 59 inches

Materials
 Plymouth Encore Worsted 75 percent acrylic/25 percent wool worsted weight yarn (200 yds/100g per ball): 11 balls medium rose #180
- Size 10 (6mm) 30-inch circular needle or size needed to obtain gauge
- Stitch markers

Gauge
24 sts and 20 rows = 4 inches/10cm in pat st
To save time, take time to check gauge.

Pattern Stitch
Mock Cable
Row 1 (RS): P3, *sl 1k, k2, psso, p2; rep from *, end last rep p3.
Row 2: K3, *p1, yo, p1, k2; rep from *, end last rep k3.
Row 3: P3, *k3, p2; rep from *, end last rep p3.
Row 4: K3, *p3, k2; rep from *, end last rep k3.
Rep Rows 1–4 for pat.

Pattern Note
Circular needle is used to accommodate large number of sts. Do not join; work in rows.

Afghan
Cast on 286 sts.
Beg with a WS row, work even in St st for 9 rows.
Turning row (RS): K17, *yo, k2tog; rep from * to last 17 sts, k17.
Work even in St st for 9 rows.
Set up pat
Next row (RS): K16, pm, work Mock Cable pat to last 16 sts, pm, k16.
Keeping sts between markers in Mock Cable pat and rem sts in St st, work even until afghan measures approx 52 inches above turning row, ending with Row 4 of pat.

Top Border
Work even in St st for 8 rows.
Turning row (RS): K17, *yo, k2tog; rep from * to last 17 sts, k17.
Work even in St st for 9 rows.
Bind off.

Finishing
Fold side border to WS, forming hem.
Sew in place.
Rep for other side.
Fold lower border to WS on turning row.
Sew in place.
Rep for top border. ∎

Mirror Image

Design by KATHLEEN SASSER

NO MORE TRYING TO FIGURE OUT WHICH SIDE IS THE RIGHT SIDE. IT'S REVERSIBLE!

Skill Level

 EASY

Finished Size
Approx 44 x 56 inches

Materials
- Plymouth Galway Worsted 100 percent wool worsted weight yarn (210 yds/100g per ball): 10 balls light blue aqua #128
- Size 7 (4.5mm) 36-inch circular needle or size needed to obtain gauge
- Stitch markers

Gauge
19 sts and 23 rows = 4 inches/10cm in Moss Diamond pat
To save time, take time to check gauge.

Pattern Stitches
A. Double Moss
Rows 1 and 2: *K1, p1; rep from * across.
Rows 3 and 4: *P1, k1; rep from * across.
Rep Rows 1–4 for pat.

B. Moss Diamond (multiple of 24 sts)
Rows 1 and 2: *K6, p6; rep from * across.
Rows 3 and 4: *P1, k5, p5, k1; rep from * across.
Rows 5 and 6: *K1, p1, k4, p4, k1, p1; rep from * across.
Rows 7 and 8: *P1, k1, p1, k3, p3, k1, p1, k1; rep from * across.
Rows 9 and 10: *[K1, p1] twice, k2, p2, [k1, p1] twice; rep from * across.
Rows 11 and 12: *P1, k1; rep from * across.

Rows 13 and 14: *K1, p1; rep from * across.
Rows 15 and 16: *[P1, k1] twice, p2, k2, [p1, k1] twice; rep from * across.
Rows 17 and 18: *K1, p1, k1, p3, k3, p1, k1, p1; rep from * across.
Rows 19 and 20: *P1, k1, p4, k4, p1, k1; rep from * across.
Rows 21 and 22: *K1, p5, k5, p1; rep from * across.
Rows 23 and 24: *P6, k6; rep from * across.
Rows 25 and 26: *P5, k1, p1, k5; rep from * across.
Rows 27 and 28: *P4, [k1, p1] twice, k4; rep from * across.
Rows 29 and 30: *P3, [k1, p1] 3 times, k3; rep from * across.
Rows 31 and 32: *P2, [k1, p1] 4 times, k2; rep from * across.
Rows 33 and 34: *P1, k1; rep from * across.
Rows 35 and 36: *K1, p1; rep from * across.
Rows 37 and 38: *K2, [p1, k1] 4 times, p2; rep from * across.
Rows 39 and 40: *K3, [p1, k1] 3 times, p3; rep from * across.
Rows 41 and 42: *K4, [p1, k1] twice, p4; rep from * across.
Rows 43 and 44: *K5, p1, k1, p5; rep from * across.
Rep Rows 1–44 for pat.

Pattern Notes
Circular needle is used to accommodate large number of sts. Do not join; work in rows.

Throw

Cast on 212 sts.

Work in Double Moss pattern for 2 inches.

Set up pat

Work 10 sts in Double Moss pat, pm, work in Moss Diamond pat to last 10 sts, pm, work 10 sts in Double Moss pat.

Work even in established pats, until 7 reps of Moss Diamond pat have been completed.

Removing markers, work Double Moss pattern across all stitches for 2 inches. Bind off in pat. ∎

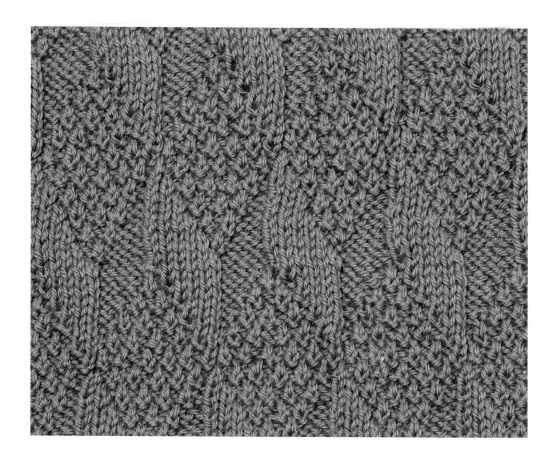

Checks & Cables Blanket

Design by ANNA AL

BLOCKS OF COLOR INGENIOUSLY TRADE PLACES

BY MEANS OF BRAIDED CABLES IN A FASCINATING

INTARSIA PROJECT.

Skill Level

■■■▢ INTERMEDIATE

Finished Size

Approx 44 x 54 inches

Materials

6 SUPER BULKY Plymouth Yukon Print 35 percent mohair/35 percent wool/30 percent acrylic super bulky weight yarn (60 yds/ 100g per skein): 8 balls lagoon #2001 (A)

6 SUPER BULKY Plymouth Yukon 35 percent mohair/35 percent wool/30 percent acrylic super bulky weight yarn (60 yds/ 100g per skein): 9 balls soft white #70 (B)

- Size 15 (10mm) 30-inch circular needle or size needed to obtain gauge
- Cable needle

Gauge

12 sts and 17 rows = 4 inches/10cm in St st

To save time, take time to check gauge.

Special Abbreviations

C8A (Cable 8 With A): Sl 4 sts to cn and hold in front, k4 A, k4 B from cn.

C8B (Cable 8 With B): Sl 4 sts to cn and hold in front, k4 B, k4 A from cn.

Pattern Notes

Circular needle is used to accommodate large number of sts. Do not join; work in rows.

Wind separate balls or bobbins for each color area.

To avoid holes when changing colors, always bring new color up over old.

Blanket

Cast on 16 with B, 18 with A, 18 with B, 18 with A, 16 with B.

Working in established color pat, knit 5 rows.

Set up pat

Inc row (RS): K14 B, [inc 1 st in next st] twice; with A, [inc 1 st in next st] twice, k14 A, [inc 1 st in next st] twice; with B, [inc 1 st in next st] twice, k14 B, [inc 1 st in next st] twice; with A, [inc 1 st in next st] twice, k14 A, [inc 1 st in next st] twice, k14 A.

Next row: P18 B, p22 A, p22 B, p22 A, p18 B.

Row 1 (RS): K14 A, C8B, k14 B, C8A, k14 A, C8B, k14 B, C8A, k14 A.

Rows 2–12: Work even in established color pat and St st.

Row 13: K14 A, C8A, k14 B, C8B, k14 A, C8A, k14 B, C8B, k14 A.

Rows 14–24: Work even in established color pat and St st.

Row 25: K14 B, C8A, k14 A, C8B, k14 B, C8A, k14 A, C8B, k14 B.

Rows 26–36: Work even in established color pat and St st.

Row 37: K14 B, C8B, k14 A, C8A, k14 B, C8B, k14 A, C8A, k14 B.

Rows 38–48: Work even in established color pat and St st.

Rep [Rows 1–48] twice, then Rows 1–24 once. (7 rows of 5 squares)

Dec row (RS): K14 B, [k2tog] twice; with A, [k2tog] twice, k14, [k2tog] twice; with B, [k2tog] twice, k14, [k2tog] twice; with A, [k2tog] twice, k14, [k2tog] twice; with B, [k2tog] twice, k14.

Working in established color pat, knit 5 rows.

Bind off knitwise in established color pat.

Side Border

With B and RS facing, pick up and knit 124 sts along 1 side edge of blanket.

Knit 5 rows.

Bind off knitwise on WS.

Rep for opposite side edge. ∎

Rainbow Squares

Design by SCARLET TAYLOR

THE JOINING SEAMS OF EASY-KNIT BLOCKS

FORM AN INTEGRAL PART OF THE DESIGN IN A

COLORFUL AFGHAN.

Skill Level

 BEGINNER

Finished Size

Approx 63 x 42 inches (excluding fringe)

Materials

6 SUPER BULKY Plymouth Rimini Rainbow 60 percent acrylic/40 percent wool super bulky weight yarn (38 yds/50g per ball): 26 balls fruit rainbow #10

- Size 13 (9mm) needles or size needed to obtain gauge
- Size L/11 (8mm) crochet hook
- Matching worsted weight yarn for seaming

Gauge

8 sts and 12 rows = 4 inches/10cm in St st
To save time, take time to check gauge.

Afghan
Basic Square
Make 24
Cast on 21 sts.

Work in St st until square measures 10½ inches, ending with a WS row. Bind off loosely.

Assembly

Lay out squares in 6 rows of 4 blocks each to form a pleasing pat.

With RS facing and matching worsted weight yarn, backstitch 6 squares tog, creating a reverse seam.

Join strips in same manner with long vertical seams.

Cut strands of yarn, each 14 inches long. Holding 3 strands tog, fold each group in half.

Working along sides of 1 square, insert crochet hook from WS to RS.

Pull fold of fringe through fabric. Draw ends through lp and fasten tightly.

Having 6 fringes along each side of each square, rep around all 4 sides of afghan.

Trim fringe evenly. ∎

Blueberry Lace

Design by SUE CHILDRESS

HOURGLASS CABLES FORM A LOVELY OPENWORK PATTERN ON A LACY AFGHAN.

Skill Level
 EASY

Finished Size
Approx 45 x 54 inches

Materials
 Plymouth Encore Chunky 75 percent acrylic/25 percent wool bulky weight yarn (143 yds/100g per ball): 9 balls blue heather #149
• Size 11 (8mm) 30-inch circular needle or size needed to obtain gauge

Gauge
10 sts and 8 rows = 4 inches/10cm in pat st
To save time, take time to check gauge.

Pattern Stitches
A. Border
Row 1 (RS): K2, *p3, k2; rep from * across.
Rows 2 and 4: Purl.
Row 3: *P3, k2; rep from * to last 2 sts, p2.
Row 5: Purl.
Row 6: Rep Row 3.
Row 7: Purl.

B. Hourglass Cables
Row 1 (RS): K2, [p3, k2] twice, k6, *p1, k5; rep from * to last 13 sts, k3, [p3, k2] twice.
Row 2: P12, k1, *p5, k1; rep from * to last 12 sts, p12.
Row 3: [P3, k2] twice, p2, k1, *yo, ssk, p1,

k2tog, yo, k1; rep from * to last 12 sts, [p3, k2] twice, p2.
Row 4: P12, k1, p2, *k1, p5; rep from * to last 16 sts, k1, p2, k1, p12.
Row 5: K2, [p3, k2] twice, k3, *p1, k5; rep from * to last 10 sts, [p3, k2] twice.
Row 6: P12, k1, p2, *k1, p5; rep from * to last 16 sts, k1, p2, k1, p12.
Row 7: [P3, k2] twice, p2, k1, *k2tog, yo, k1, yo, ssk, p1; rep from * to last 18 sts, k2tog, yo, k1, yo, ssk, k1, [p3, k2] twice, p2.
Row 8: P12, k1, [p5, k1] to last 12 sts, p12
Rep Rows 1–8 for pat.

Pattern Note
Circular needle is used to accommodate large number of sts. Do not join; work in rows.

Afghan
Cast on 137 sts.
Knit 1 row.
Work 7 rows of Border pat.
Inc row: Purl in front and back of first st, purl to last stitch, purl in front and back of last st. (139 sts)
[Work Rows 1–8 of Hourglass Cables pat] 22 times; rep Rows 1–7.
Dec row: P2tog, p10, k1, *p5, k1; rep from * to last 12 sts, p10, p2tog. (137 sts)
Work Rows 1– 7 of Border pat.
Purl 1 row, knit 1 row.
Bind off. ■

Shadow Stitch Stripes

Design by CAROL MAY

SUBTLE STRIPES CREATE A COZY THROW.

Skill Level
 INTERMEDIATE

Finished Size
Approx 40 x 50 inches

Materials
 Plymouth Encore Worsted 75 percent acrylic/25 percent wool worsted weight yarn (200 yds/100g per ball): 6 balls medium brown #1204 (A), 4 balls dark brown #599 (B), 2 balls aran #256 (C)
- Size 7 (4.5mm) 30-inch circular needle or size needed to obtain gauge
- 4 bobbins for cables
- Stitch markers
- Cable needle

Gauge
20 sts and 20 rows = 4 inches/10cm in pat st
To save time, take time to check gauge.

Pattern Stitches
A. Cables (panel of 5 sts, worked with A)
Rows 1 and 5 (RS): Knit.
Row 2 and all WS rows: Purl.
Row 3: Sl 2 sts to cn and hold in front, k3, k2 from cn.
Rep Rows 1–6 for pat.

B. Stripe (panel of 36 sts)
Row 1 (RS): With B, *k3, p3; rep from * across.
Row 2: With B, purl.
Row 3: With A, *p3, k3; rep from * across.
Row 4: With A, purl.
Rep Rows 1–4 for pat.

C. Checks (panel of 35 sts)
Rows 1 and 5 (RS): With C, p5, *k5, p5; rep from * across.
Row 2 and all WS rows: Purl with color of previous row.
Rows 3 and 7: With A, k5, *p5, k5; rep from * across.
Row 9: With C, purl.
Rows 11 and 15: With A, p5, *k5, p5; rep from * across.
Rows 13 and 17: With C, k5, *p5, k5; rep from * across.
Row 19: With A, purl.
Row 20: Rep Row 2.
Rep Rows 1–20 for pat.

Pattern Notes
Throw is worked in one piece.
Circular needle is used to accommodate large number of sts. Do not join; work in rows.
All WS rows are purled with color used in previous row.
Use separate balls of yarn for each color area. Wind 4 smaller separate bobbins (1 for each cable panel)
To avoid holes when changing colors, always bring new color up over old.

Throw
With A, cast on 198 sts.
Purl 5 rows.
Next row (WS): [P36, pm, p5, pm, p35, pm, p5, pm] twice, p36.
Set up pat (RS): Work Row 1 of [Stripe panel, Cable panel, Checks panel, Cable panel] twice, Stripe panel.
Work even in established pats until throw measures approx 55 inches, ending with Row 17 of Checks panel.
With A, purl 6 rows.
Bind off loosely. ■

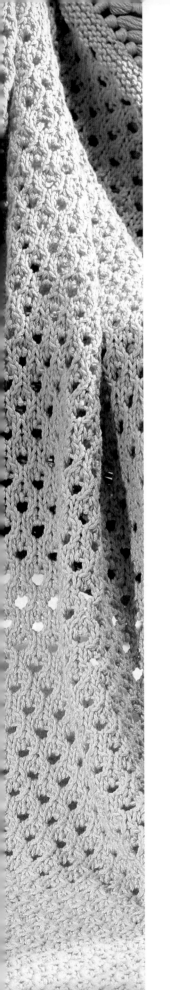

Serene Seas

Design by LOIS S. YOUNG

A GENTLE COLOR AND EASY PATTERN ARE USED IN A SUMMER AFGHAN. DOUBLE-KNOTTED FRINGE ADDS A FINISHING TOUCH.

Skill Level
■■□□ EASY

Finished Size
Approx 42 x 58 inches

Materials
 Plymouth Fantasy Naturale 100 percent mercerized cotton worsted weight yarn (140 yds/100g per hank): 13 hanks sea green #5425
- Size 8 (5mm) 30-inch circular needle or size needed to obtain gauge
- Size G/6 (4mm) crochet hook

Gauge
15 sts and 16 rows = 4 inches/10cm in Sea Foam pat
To save time, take time to check gauge.

Pattern Stitch
Sea Foam
Row 1 (RS): Sl 1, k4, *k2tog, [yo] twice, ssk; rep from * to last 5 sts, k5.
Rows 2 and 6: Sl 1, k4, purl to last 5 sts, k5.
Rows 3 and 7: Sl 1, knit to end of row.
Rows 4 and 8: Sl 1, k4, purl to last 5 sts, k5.
Row 5: Sl 1, k4, *yo, ssk, k2tog, yo; rep from * to last 5 sts, k5.
Rep Rows 1–8 for pat.

Pattern Notes
Circular needle is used to accommodate large number of sts. Do not join; work in rows.
Slip first st of each row purlwise.
On Rows 2 and 6 of pat, work (p1, k1) into each double yo.

Afghan
Cast on 145 sts.
Knit 9 rows, slipping first st of every row.
Work even in Sea Foam pat until afghan measures approx 57 inches, ending with Row 3 of pat.
Knit 9 rows.
Bind off knitwise on WS.

Tasseled Fringe
Cut strands of yarn, each 18 inches long.
Holding 4 strands tog, pull through every other st along cast-on edge.
Adjust strands evenly and tie each group in an overhand knot.
With same group of strands, tie another overhand knot 1 inch below first.
Rep along bound-off edge.
Trim fringe evenly. ■

A Splash of Summer

Design by KATHARINE HUNT

THE DEEP BLUE OF A LAKE OR POND IS CAPTURED IN AN AFGHAN WITH A WAVE AND DIAMOND PATTERN.

Skill Level

 INTERMEDIATE

Finished Size

Approx 46 x 55 inches

Materials

 Plymouth Encore Worsted 75 percent acrylic/25 percent wool worsted weight yarn (200 yds/100g per ball): 11 balls turquoise #235
- Size 6 (4mm) 30-inch circular needle or size needed to obtain gauge
- Stitch markers

Gauge

20 sts and 28 rows = 4 inches/10cm in pat st
To save time, take time to check gauge.

Pattern Stitch

Double Moss

Row 1 (RS): *K1, p1; rep from * across.
Rows 2 and 4: Knit the knit sts and purl the purl sts as they present themselves.
Row 3: *P1, k1; rep from * across.
Rep Rows 1–4 for pat.

Pattern Notes

Circular needle is used to accommodate large number of sts. Do not join; work in rows.
Side borders are worked with the body. They are 10 stitches wide, consisting of 7 sts in Double Moss pat on the outside, plus 3 sts in St st adjacent to the body.
To keep the edges of the side borders neat,
give an extra tug before and after working each edge stitch.
Chart is read from right to left on RS rows, and left to right on WS rows.
Pay close attention to spacing on either side of openwork panel on chart; it varies between 5 and 6 sts. These are marked with a red *.

Afghan

Cast on 235 sts.
Knit 3 rows.
Preparation row (WS): Referring to chart and reading from left to right, work from D to B once, pm for border, work from C to A once, then [B to A] 3 times, pm for border, work from B to D once.
Referring to chart [Rep Rows 1– 28] 13 times, ending with Row 25 on last rep.
Knit 2 rows.
Bind off on WS.

Top & Bottom Edging

Make 2

Cast on 8 sts.
Row 1 (RS): Sl 1k, k2, yo, k2tog, [yo] twice, k2tog, k1. (9 sts)
Row 2: K3, p1, k2, yo, k2tog, k1.
Row 3: Sl 1, k2, yo, k2tog, k1, [yo] twice, k2tog, k1. (10 sts)
Row 4: K3, p1, k3, yo, k2tog, k1.
Row 5: Sl 1, k2, yo, k2tog, k2, [yo] twice, k2tog, k1. (11 sts)
Row 6: K3, p1, k4, yo, k2tog, k1.
Row 7: Sl 1, k2, yo, k2tog, k6.
Row 8: Bind off 3 sts knitwise (1 st rems on RH needle), k4, yo, k2tog, k1. (8 sts)

Rep Rows 1–8 until edging, when slightly stretched, measures same as cast-on or bound-off edge. End with Row 8 of pat.

Next row: *K1, p1; rep from * across. Bind off.

Assembly

Sew 1 edging to top of afghan. Rep for rem edging. ■

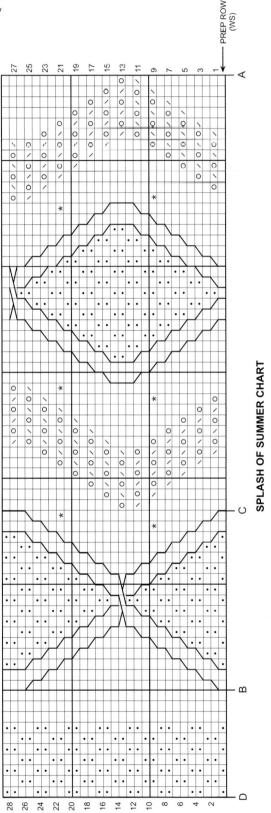

SPLASH OF SUMMER CHART

STITCH KEY
- ☐ K on RS, p on WS
- · P on RS, k on WS
- ○ Yo
- ＼ Ssk
- ／ K2tog
- ✕✕✕ Sl 3 to cn and hold in back, K2, sl last st from cn to LH needle & knit it. K2 from cn.

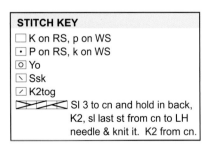

Diamonds in Denim

Design by SANDI PROSSER

A CASUAL THROW IN EASY-CARE COTTON AND DENIM
COLORS WOULD MAKE AN INDISPENSABLE ADDITION TO
A COLLEGE DORM ROOM.

Skill Level
 **INTERMEDIATE**

Finished Size
Approx 43 x 53 inches

Materials
[4 MEDIUM] Plymouth Fantasy Naturale 100
percent mercerized cotton worsted
weight yarn (140 yds/100g per skein): 13
skeins denim #8003
- Size 9 (5.5mm) 30-inch circular needle or
size needed to obtain gauge

Gauge
16 sts and 21 rows = 4 inches/10cm in
St st
To save time, take time to check gauge.

Pattern Stitch
Diamonds
Row 1 (RS): Knit.

Row 2: K6, purl to last 6 sts, k6.

Row 3: K14, *k2tog, yo, k1, yo, ssk, k15;
rep from * 6 times, k2tog, yo, k1, yo, ssk,
k14.

Row 4: K6, p10, *k1, p19; rep from * 6
times, k1, p10, k6.

Row 5: K13, *k2tog, yo, k1, p1, k1, yo,
ssk, k13; rep from * 7 times.

Row 6: K6, p9, *k1, p1, k1, p17; rep from
* 6 times, k1, p1, k1, p9, k6.

Row 7: K12, *k2tog, yo, [k1, p1] twice, k1,
yo, ssk, k11; rep from * 6 times, k2tog, yo,
[k1, p1] twice, k1, yo, ssk, k12.

Row 8: K6, p8, *[k1, p1] twice, k1, p15;
rep from * 6 times, [k1, p1] twice, k1,
p8, k6.

Row 9: K11, *k2tog, yo, [k1, p1] 3 times,
k1, yo, ssk, k9; rep from * 6 times, k2tog,
yo, [k1, p1] 3 times, k1, yo, ssk, k11.

Row 10: K6, p7, *[k1, p1] 3 times, k1,
p13; rep from * 6 times, [k1, p1] 3 times,
k1, p7, k6.

Row 11: K10, *k2tog, yo, [k1, p1] 4 times,
k1, yo, ssk, k7; rep from * 6 times, k2tog,
yo, [k1, p1] 4 times, k1, yo, ssk, k10.

Row 12: K6, p6, *[k1, p1] 4 times, k1,
p11; rep from * 6 times, [k1, p1] 4 times,
k1, p6, k6.

Row 13: K9, *k2tog, yo, [k1, p1] 5 times,
k1, yo, ssk, k5; rep from * 6 times, k2tog,
yo, [k1, p1] 5 times, k1, yo, ssk, k9.

Row 14: K6, p5, *[k1, p1] 5 times, k1,
p9; rep from * 6 times, [k1, p1] 5 times, k1,
p5, k6.

Row 15: K8, *k2tog, yo, [k1, p1] 6 times,
k1, yo, ssk, k3; rep from * 6 times, k2tog,
yo, [k1, p1] 6 times, k1, yo, ssk, k8.

Row 16: K6, p4, *[k1, p1] 6 times, k1, p7;
rep from * 6 times, [k1, p1] 6 times, k1,
p4, k6.

Row 17: K7, *k2tog, yo, [k1, p1] 7 times,
k1, yo, ssk, k1; rep from * 6 times, k2tog,
yo, [k1, p1] 7 times, k1, yo, ssk, k7.

Row 18: K6, p3, *[k1, p1] 7 times, k1,
p5; rep from * 6 times, [k1, p1] 7 times, k1,
p3, k6.

Row 19: K7, *yo, ssk, k15, k2tog, yo, k1;
rep from * 7 times, k6.

Row 20: K7, *p19, k1; rep from * 7 times, k6.

Row 21: K6, p1, k1, *yo, ssk, k13, k2tog, yo, k1, p1, k1; rep from * 6 times, yo, ssk, k13, k2tog, yo, k1, p1, k6.

Row 22: K6, p1, k1, p17, *k1, p1, k1, p17; rep from * 6 times, k1, p1, k6.

Row 23: K7, p1, k1, *yo, ssk, k11, k2tog, yo, k1, [p1, k1] twice; rep from * 6 times, yo, ssk, k11, k2tog, yo, k1, p1, k7.

Row 24: K7, p1, k1, p15, *k1, [p1, k1] twice, p15; rep from * 6 times, k1, p1, k7.

Row 25: K6, [p1, k1] twice, *yo, ssk, k9, k2tog, yo, k1, [p1, k1] 3 times; rep from * 6 times, yo, ssk, k9, k2tog, yo, [k1, p1] twice, k6.

Row 26: K6, [p1, k1] twice, p13, *k1, [p1, k1] 3 times, p13; rep from * 6 times, [k1, p1] twice, k6.

Row 27: K7, [p1, k1] twice, *yo, ssk, k7, k2tog, yo, k1, [p1, k1] 4 times; rep from * 6 times, yo, ssk, k7, k2tog, yo, [k1, p1] twice, k7.

Row 28: K7, [p1, k1] twice, p11, *k1, [p1, k1] 4 times, p11; rep from * 6 times, [k1, p1] twice, k7.

Row 29: K6, [p1, k1] 3 times, *yo, ssk, k5, k2tog, yo, k1, [p1, k1] 5 times; rep from * 6 times, yo, ssk, k5, k2tog, yo, [k1, p1] 3 times, k6.

Row 30: K6, [p1, k1] 3 times, p9, *k1, [p1, k1] 5 times, p9; rep from * 6 times, [k1, p1] 3 times, k6.

Row 31: K7, [p1, k1] 3 times, *yo, ssk, k3, k2tog, yo, k1, [p1, k1] 6 times, rep from * 6 times, yo, ssk, k3, k2tog, yo, [k1, p1] 3 times, k7.

Row 32: K7, [p1, k1] 3 times, p7, *k1, [p1, k1] 6 times, p7; rep from * 6 times, [k1, p1] 3 times, k7.

Row 33: K6, [p1, k1] 4 times, *yo, ssk, k1, k2tog, yo, k1, [p1, k1] 7 times; rep from * 6 times, yo, ssk, k1, k2tog, yo, [k1, p1] 4 times, k6.

Row 34: K6, [p1, k1] 4 times, p5, *k1, [p1, k1] 6 times, p5; rep from * 6 times, [k1, p1] 4 times, k6.

Rep Rows 3–34 for pat.

Pattern Note

Circular needle is used to accommodate large number of sts. Do not join; work in rows.

Throw

Cast on 174 sts.

Beg with a WS row, knit 7 rows.

Work even in Diamonds pat until throw measures approx 52 inches, ending with Row 18 or 34 of pat.

Knit 7 rows.

Bind off knitwise. ■

Blue Lover's Dream

Design by CAROL MAY

DELICATE SHADES OF BLUE AND WHITE COMBINE WITH SLIP STITCHES TO CREATE AN EMBROIDERED LOOK ON A HEAVENLY THROW.

Skill Level

■■■□ **INTERMEDIATE**

Finished Size

Approx 44 x 50 inches

Materials

4 MEDIUM Plymouth Encore Worsted 75 percent acrylic/25 percent wool worsted weight yarn (200 yds/100g per ball): 3 balls dark blue #598 (A), 5 balls medium blue #515 (B), 5 balls white #208 (C)
- Size 7 (4.5mm) 30-inch circular needle or size needed to obtain gauge
- Size H/8 (5mm) crochet hook

Gauge

21 sts and 26 rows = 4 inches/10cm in pat st
To save time, take time to check gauge.

Special Abbreviation

Lift: Place right needle under lp of contrasting yarn and continue with knit st of base color.

Pattern Notes

Circular needle is used to accommodate large number of sts. Do not join; work in rows.
When a RS row follows a RS row, slide sts to opposite end of needle.
When slipping 5 sts, bring yarn over thumb to make loose lp.

Throw

With A, cast on 238 sts.
Knit 10 rows. Cut yarn.

**Blue Section

Row 1 (RS): With B, knit. Slide.
Row 2 (RS): With C, sl 2, bring yarn to front, *sl 5 wyif, p1; rep from *, end last rep sl 2 wyib. Cut C.
Rows 3 and 5 (WS): With B, purl.
Row 4 (RS): With B, knit.
Row 6 (RS): With B, *k5, lift C while knitting B; rep from *, end last rep k5. Slide.
Row 7 (RS): With C, sl 5, bring yarn to front of work, *p1 wyif, sl 5; rep from * to last 5 sts, sl 5 wyib. Cut C.
Rows 8 and 10 (WS): With B, purl.
Row 9 (RS): With B, knit.
Row 11 (RS): With B, k2, *lift C while knitting B, k5; rep from * to last 2 sts, k2. Slide.
Row 12 (RS): With C, sl 2, *p1 wyif, sl 5; rep from * to last 2 sts, sl 2 wyib.
Rep these 12 rows twice.***
Beg with a RS row, knit 6 rows A.

White Section

Row 1 (RS): With C, knit. Slide.
Row 2 (RS): With B, sl 2, bring yarn to front, *sl 5 wyif, p1; rep from * to last 2 sts, sl 2 wyib. Cut B.
Rows 3 and 5 (WS): With C, purl.
Row 6 (RS): With C, *k5, lift B while knitting C; rep from * to last 5 sts, k5. Slide.
Row 7 (RS): With B, sl 5, bring yarn to

front, *p1 wyif, sl 5; rep from * to last 5 sts, sl 5 wyib. Cut B.

Rows 8 and 10 (WS): With C, purl.

Row 9 (RS): With C, knit.

Row 11 (RS): With C, k2 *lift B while knitting C, k5; rep from * to last 2 sts, k2. Slide.

Row 12 (RS): With B, sl 2, *p1 wyif, sl 5; rep from * to last 2 sts, sl 2 wyib.

Rep these 12 rows twice.

Beg with a RS row, knit 6 rows A.^^

Rep from ** to ** 3 times; rep from ** to *** once.

Knit 10 rows A.

Bind off loosely.

Fringe

Cut strands of yarn, each 10 inches long.

Holding 2 strands tog, fold each group in half.

Working along side edge, insert crochet hook from WS to RS.

Pull fold of fringe through fabric. Draw ends through lp and fasten tightly.

Alternating groups of B and C, attach 12 groups in each wide section.

Attach 2 groups of A in each garter-st section between wide bands, and 3 groups in each end section.

Rep along opposite edge.

Trim fringe evenly. ■

Slip Stitch Diamonds & Cables

Design by SANDI PROSSER

MOSAIC PANELS ALTERNATE WITH CABLES IN A

DRAMATIC THROW.

Skill Level
 EASY

Finished Size
Approx 39 x 46 inches

Materials
 Plymouth Indiecita Suri Merino 55 percent Suri Alpaca/45 percent extrafine merino worsted weight yarn (109 yds/50g ball): 12 balls garnet #2055 (MC), 8 balls black #500 (CC)
- Size 7 (4.5mm) needles or size needed to obtain gauge
- Cable needle

Gauge
20 sts and 28 rows = 4 inches/10cm in St st
To save time, take time to check gauge.

Pattern Note
Sl all sts purlwise, with yarn to WS of work

Throw
Diamond Panel
Make 3
With MC, cast on 53 sts.
Knit 1 row.
Row 1 (RS): With CC, k1, [k1, sl 1] 3 times, k7, *sl 1, [k1, sl 1] 4 times, k7; rep from * to last 7 sts, [sl 1, k1] 3 times, k1.
Row 2: Rep Row 1.
Rows 3 and 4: With MC, k7, sl 1, [k1, sl 1] 3 times, *k9, sl 1, [k1, sl 1] 3 times; rep from * to last 7 sts, k7.
Rows 5 and 6: With CC, k1, [k1, sl 1] twice, k5, sl 1, k5, *sl 1, [k1, sl 1] twice, k5, sl 1, k5; rep from * to last 5 sts, [sl 1, k1] twice, k1.
Rows 7 and 8: With MC, *k5, sl 1, k1, sl 1; rep from * to last 5 sts, k5.
Rows 9 and 10: With CC, k2, sl 1, *k5, sl 1, [k1, sl 1] twice, k5, sl 1; rep from * to last 2 sts, k2.
Rows 11 and 12: With MC, k3, sl 1, k1, sl 1, k9, *sl 1, [k1, sl 1] 3 times, k9; rep from * to last 6 sts, sl 1, k1, sl 1, k3.
Rows 13 and 14: With CC, k6, sl 1, [k1, sl 1] 4 times, *k7, sl 1, [k1, sl 1] 4 times; rep from * to last 6 sts, k6.
Rows 15 and 16: With MC, k3, sl 1, k13, *sl 1, k1, sl 1, k13; rep from * to last 4 sts, sl 1, k3.
Rows 17 and 18: Rep Rows 13 and 14.
Rows 19 and 20: Rep Rows 11 and 12.
Rows 21 and 22: Rep Rows 9 and 10.
Rows 23 and 24: Rep Rows 7 and 8.
Rows 25 and 26: Rep Rows 5 and 6.
Rows 27 and 28: Rep Rows 3 and 4.
[Rep Rows 1–28] 15 times; rep Rows 1 and 2.
With MC, knit 2 rows.
Bind off purlwise.

Cable Panel
Make 4
With MC, cast on 16 sts.

Knit 1 row.

Rows 1, 3, 5, 7 and 9 (RS): Knit.

Row 2 and all WS rows: K3, p10, k3.

Row 11: K3, sl 5 sts to cn and hold in back, k5, k5 from cn, k3.

Row 12: Rep Row 2.

[Rep Rows 1–12] 26 times; rep Rows 1–9.

Knit 1 row.

Bind off purlwise.

Assembly

Sew panels tog, alternating Diamond and Cable panels as shown in photo.

Fringe

Cut strands of yarn, each 12 inches long.

Holding 3 strands tog, fold each group in half.

Working along cast-on edge, insert crochet hook from WS to RS.

Pull fold of fringe through fabric. Draw ends through lp and fasten tightly.

Four groups of MC are worked in each Cable panel, 11 groups of CC are worked in each diamond panel.

Rep along bound-off edge.

Trim fringe evenly. ■

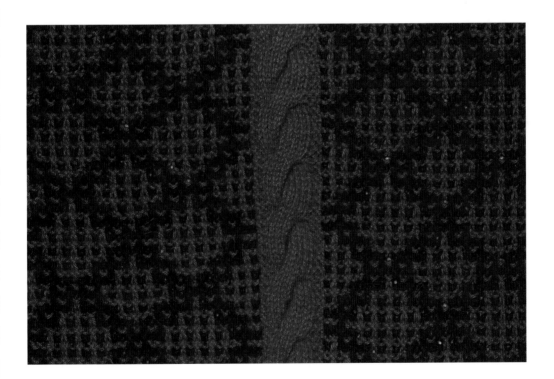

Long Rib Cables

Design by SANDI PROSSER

SOFT-AS-BUTTER ALPACA YARN IS FASHIONED INTO A
THROW WITH SPECTACULAR RIBBED CABLES.

Skill Level

 INTERMEDIATE

Finished Size
Approx 43 x 47 inches

Materials
 Plymouth Indiecita Alpaca Suri
Merino 55 percent Suri Alpaca/45
percent extra fine merino worsted
weight yarn (109 yds/50g per ball):
20 balls naturale #100
- Size 7 (4.5mm) 30-inch circular needle
  or size needed to obtain gauge
- Cable needle

Gauge
20 sts and 28 rows = 4 inches/10cm in
St st
To save time, take time to check gauge.

Special Abbreviations
C9B (Cable 9 Back): Sl 4 sts to cn and
and hold in back, k5, k4 from cn.
C9F (Cable 9 Front): Sl 5 sts to cn and
hold in front, k4, k5 from cn.
K1B (Knit 1 Below): Knit the st 1 row
below the st on LH needle, sl top st off
needle without working it.

Pattern Stitch
Long Cable
Row 1 (WS): K3, *p5, k1 [p1, k1] 4 times,
p5, k2, p5, k1, [p1, k1] 4 times, p5, k2; rep
from * to last st, k1.

Row 2: K1, p2, *k5, p1, [K1B, p1] 4 times,
k5, p2, k5, p1, [K1B, p1] 4 times, k5, p2;
rep from * to last st, k1.
Rows 3–13: Rep Rows 1 and 2.
Row 14: K1, p2, *C9B, p1, C9F, p2, k5,
p1, [K1B, p1] 4 times, k5, p2; rep from * to
last st, k1.
Row 15: K3, *p5, k1 [p1, k1] 4 times, p5,
k2, p9, k1, p9, k2; rep from * to last st, k1.
Row 16: K1, p2, *k9, p1, k9, p2, k5, p1,
[K1B, p1] 4 times, k5, p2; rep from * to last
st, k1.
Rows 17–23: Rep Rows 15 and 16.
Row 24: Rep Row 14.
Rows 25–39: Rep Rows 1 and 2.
Row 40: K1, p2, *k5, p1, [K1B, p1] 4
times, k5, p2, C9B, p1, C9F, p2; rep from *
to last st, k1.
Row 41: K3, *p9, k1, p9, p5, k1 [p1, k1] 4
times, p5, k2,; rep from * to last st, k1.
Row 42: K1, p2, *k5, p1, [K1B, p1] 4
times, k5, p2, k9, p1, k9, p2; rep from * to
last st, k1.
Rows 43–49: Rep Rows 41 and 42.
Row 50: Rep Row 40.
Rep Rows 1–50 for pat.

Pattern Note
Circular needle is used to accommodate
large number of sts. Do not join; work
in rows.

Throw
Cast on 256 sts.
Work even in Long Cable pat until throw
measures approx 47 inches, ending with
Row 37 of pat.
Bind off in pat.

Fringe

Cut strands of yarn, each 12 inches long.
Holding 5 strands tog, fold each group in half.
Working along cast-on edge, insert crochet
hook from WS to RS in center st of each
cable motif.

Pull fold of fringe through fabric. Draw ends
through lp and fasten tightly.
Rep along bound-off edge.
Trim fringe evenly. ■

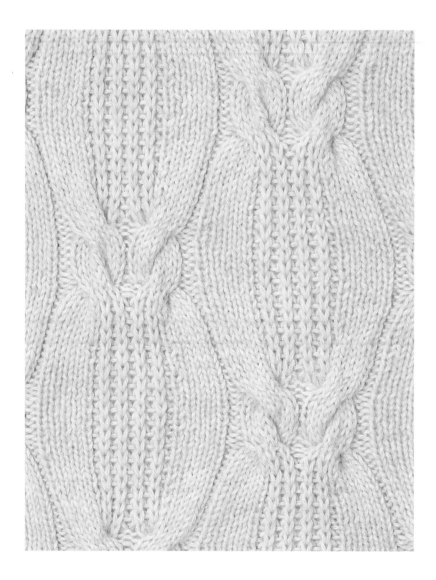

Reversible Riot of Color

Design by COLLEEN SMITHERMAN

THIS REVERSIBLE AFGHAN IS ALIVE WITH COLOR AND
TEXTURE. WORKING IN SEPARATE PANELS MAKES IT A
CONVENIENTLY PORTABLE PROJECT.

Skill Level

 INTERMEDIATE

Finished Size
Approx 48 x 58 inches

Materials
Plymouth Encore Worsted 75
percent acrylic/25 percent wool
worsted weight yarn (200 yds/100g per
ball): 2 balls each coral #137 (A), yellow
#1014 (B), lime #3335 (C), blue #4045
(D), lavender #9624 (E)
- Size 9 (5.5mm) needles or size needed
  to obtain gauge
- Cable needle
- Stitch markers

Gauge
20 stitches and 26 rows = 4 inches/10cm in
cable pat
To save time, take time to check gauge.

Afghan
Center Panel
Make 1 each A, B and C
Cast on 48 sts.
Lower Border
Row 1 (RS): K1, [p2, k2] 11 times, p2, k1.
Row 2: P1, [k2, p2] 11 times, k2, p1.

[Rep Rows 1 and 2] 6 times.
Referring to chart and working from A to
D, work even until panel measures approx
54 inches, ending with a WS row between
cabled sections.
Upper Border
Row 1 (RS): K1, [p2, k2] 11 times, p2, k1.
Row 2: P1, [k2, p2] 11 times, k2, p1.
[Rep Rows 1 and 2] 6 times.
Bind off in pat.

Right Panel
With D, cast on 49 sts.
Row 1 (RS): [K2, p2] 12 times, k1.
Row 2: P1, [k2, p2] 12 times.
[Rep Rows 1 and 2] 6 times.
Next row: K2, [p2, k2] twice, pm, referring
to chart, work Row 1 from B to D.
Work even in established pat until cabled
section measures same as center panels.
Upper Border
Row 1 (RS): [K2, p2] 12 times, k1.
Row 2: P1, [k2, p2] 12 times.
[Rep Rows 1 and 2] 6 times.
Bind off in pat.

Left Panel
With E, cast on 49 sts.
Row 1 (RS): K1, [p2, k2] 12 times.
Row 2: [P2, k2] 12 times, p1.

[Rep Rows 1 and 2] 6 times.
Next row (RS): Referring to chart, work
Row 1 from A to C, pm, k2, [p2, k2]
2 times.
Work even in established pat until cabled
section measures same as center panels.

Upper Border
Row 1 (RS): K1, [p2, k2] 12 times.
Row 2: [K2, p2] 12 times, p1.
[Rep Rows 1 and 2] 6 times. Bind off in pat.

Assembly
Referring to photo for color placement, sew
panels tog. ■

STITCH KEY
☐	K on RS, p on WS
–	P on RS, k on WS
↗ ☐ ↘	Sl 2 to cn and hold in back, k2, k2 from cn
↘ ☐ ↙	Sl 2 to cn and hold in front, k2, k2 from cn

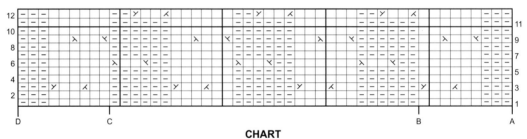

CHART
Reversible Riot of Color

Lilacs in Bloom

Design by SHARI HAUX

WRAP A BABY IN LUXURY WITH A CUDDLY ALPACA AFGHAN IN A SOFT LILAC SHADE. AN ADDED BONUS— IT'S REVERSIBLE.

Skill Level

 BEGINNER

Finished Size
Approx 43 x 43 inches

Materials
 Plymouth Baby Alpaca Grande 100 percent baby alpaca bulky weight yarn (110 yds/100g per skein): 8 skeins lavender #1830
- Size 11 (8mm) 24-inch circular needle or size needed to obtain gauge
- Stitch markers

Gauge
12 sts and 16 rows = 4 inches/10cm in Tiny Block pat
To save time, take time to check gauge.

Pattern Stitch
Tiny Blocks
Rows 1 and 2: *K2, p2; rep from * across.
Rows 3 and 4: *P2, k2; rep from * across.
Rep Rows 1–4 for pat.

Afghan
Cast on 116 sts.
Work in garter st for 10 rows.
Set up pat:
K10, pm, work in Tiny Blocks pat to last 10 sts, pm, k10.
Keeping sts between markers in Tiny Blocks pat and rem sts in garter st, work even until afghan measures approx 41 inches, ending with Row 2 or 4 of pat.
Knit 10 rows.
Bind off. ∎

Checks & Stripes Throw

Design by SANDI PROSSER

THIS SERENE THROW CONJURES UP AN IMAGE OF WOVEN RIBBONS. TRY WORKING IT IN BLACK AND WHITE FOR A MORE DRAMATIC LOOK.

Skill Level

 **INTERMEDIATE**

Finished Size
Approx 41 x 48 inches

Materials
 Plymouth Encore Worsted 75 percent acrylic/25 percent wool worsted weight yarn (200 yds/100g per ball): 4 balls each soft white #146 (A) and cornflower #4045 (B)
- Size 8 (5mm) 30-inch circular needle or size needed to obtain gauge

Gauge
16 sts and 28 rows = 4 inches/10cm in color pat
To save time, take time to check gauge.

Pattern Stitch
Checks & Stripes
Row 1 (RS): Knit.
Row 2: Purl.
Row 3: With B, k13,*[sl 1, k1] 5 times, sl 1, k11; rep from * to last 2 sts, k2.
Row 4: With B, k1, p12,*[sl 1, k1] 5 times, sl 1, p11; rep from * to last 2 sts, p1, k1.
Rows 5–12: Rep Rows 1–4.
Row 13: With A, knit.
Row 14: With A, purl.

Row 15: With B, k1, [k1, sl 1] 6 times, *k11, [sl 1, k1] 5 times, sl 1; rep from * to last 2 sts, k2.
Row 16: With B, k1, p1, [sl 1, k1] 5 times, sl 1, *p11, [sl 1, k1] 5 times, sl 1; rep from * to last 2 sts, p1, k1.
Rows 17–24: Rep Rows 13–16.
Rep Rows 1–24 for pat.

Pattern Notes
Circular needle is used to accommodate large number of sts. Do not join; work in rows.
Sl all sts purlwise, with yarn to WS of work.

Throw
With A, cast on 168 sts.
[Work Rows 1–24 of Checks & Stripes pat] 13 times.
With A, knit 1 row, purl 1 row.
Bind off.

Borders
With B, pick up and knit 168 sts along cast-on edge.
Knit 6 rows.
Bind off knitwise.
Rep along bound-off edge.
Work side borders in same manner, picking up and knitting 235 sts. ■

Velvet Stripes Lap Robe

Design by Lois S. Young

SENSUOUS VELVET STRIPES ALTERNATE WITH DELICATE OPENWORK ROWS IN A RICHLY COLORED LAP ROBE.

Skill Level

 EASY

Finished Size

Approx 36 x 46 inches (excluding fringe)

Materials

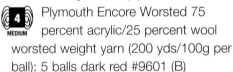 Plymouth Sinsation 80 percent rayon/20 percent wool chenille bulky weight yarn (38 yds/50g per ball): 17 balls ruby #4475 (A)

Plymouth Encore Worsted 75 percent acrylic/25 percent wool worsted weight yarn (200 yds/100g per ball): 5 balls dark red #9601 (B)

- Size 10 (6mm) 29-inch circular needle or size needed to obtain gauge
- Size Q (16mm) crochet hook

Gauge

12 sts and 20 rows = 4 inches/10cm in pat
To save time, take time to check gauge.

Pattern Stitch

Velvet Stripes

Rows 1(RS)–8: With A, sl 1p, knit to end of row.

Row 9: With B, sl 1p, knit to end of row.

Rows 10 and 12: Sl 1p, k2, purl to last 3 sts, k3.

Row 11: Sl 1p, k2, *yo, k2tog; rep from * to last 2 sts, k2.

Rep Rows 1–12 for pat.

Pattern Notes

Chenille part of afghan should be knitted as tightly as possible to prevent chenille from "worming."

Two strands of B are held tog for entire lap robe, except for fringe.

Lap Robe

With A, loosely cast on 113 sts.
Slipping first st of every row purlwise, work in garter st for 7 rows.
[Work Rows 1–12 of Velvet Stripes pat] 20 times.
Rep Rows 1–7.
Bind off knitwise on WS.

Fringe

Cut strands of B, each 14 inches long.
Holding 3 strands tog, fold each group in half.
Working along cast-on edge, insert crochet hook from WS to RS (adding two fringe for every three stitches).
Pull fold of fringe through fabric. Draw ends through lp and fasten tightly.
Rep along bound-off edge.
Trim fringe even. ■

Seeing Stars

Design by JOYCE ENGLUND

TINY STARS ABOUND ON A COLORFUL LAP ROBE.

THE SIZE ALSO MAKES IT SUITABLE FOR A CHILD.

Skill Level

 EASY

Finished Size

Approx 34 x 44 inches

Materials

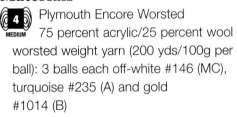 Plymouth Encore Worsted 75 percent acrylic/25 percent wool worsted weight yarn (200 yds/100g per ball): 3 balls each off-white #146 (MC), turquoise #235 (A) and gold #1014 (B)
- Size 10 (6mm) 30-inch circular needle or size needed to obtain gauge
- Stitch markers

Gauge

19 sts and 22 rows = 4 inches/10cm in Star pat
To save time, take time to check gauge.

Special Abbreviations

Make Star: P3tog leaving sts on needle, yo, then purl same 3 sts tog again.
M1 (Make 1): Make a backward lp and place on RH needle.

Pattern Stitches

A. Seed

Row 1: K1, *p1, k1; rep from * across.
All following rows: Knit the purl sts, and purl the knit sts as they present themselves.

B. Star (multiple of 4 sts + 1)

Rows 1 and 3 (RS): Knit.

Row 2: P1, Make Star, p1; rep from * across.
Row 4: P3, Make Star, *p1, Make Star; rep from * to last 3 sts, p3.
Rep Rows 1–4 for pat.

C. Color Sequence

Work 2 rows each of A, B, A, MC, B, A, B, MC.

Pattern Note

Circular needle is used to accommodate large number of sts. Do not join; work in rows.

Lap Robe

With MC, cast on 151 sts.
Work in Seed pat for 8 rows.
Inc row (WS): Work 6 sts in Seed pat, pm, k1, M1, *k2, M1; rep from * to last 6 sts, pm, work 6 sts in Seed pat.
Keeping first and last 6 sts in MC and Seed pat, and rem sts in Star pat and color sequence, work even until lap robe measures approx 42½ inches, ending with A and Row 3 of pat.
Dec row (WS): With MC, work 6 sts in Seed pat, remove marker, *p1, p2tog; rep from * to last 7 sts, k1, remove marker, work 6 sts in Seed pat.
Work 8 rows of Seed pat.
Bind off in pat. ■

Luxury Lap Afghan

Design by LYNDA ROPER

WRAP YOURSELF IN LUXURY WITH THIS COMBINATION OF SOFT AND SILKY YARNS.

Skill Level
■■□□ EASY

Finished Size
Approx 36 x 36 inches

Materials
 Plymouth Firenze 40 percent nylon/30 percent wool/30 percent acrylic bulky weight eyelash yarn (55 yds/50g per ball): 7 balls purple/blue #445 (MC)

 Plymouth Flash 100 percent nylon worsted weight eyelash yarn (190 yds/50g per ball): 4 balls soft white #900 (CC)

- Size 11 (8mm) 24-inch circular needle or size needed to obtain gauge

Gauge
11½ sts and 20 rows = 4 inches/10cm in St st
To save time, take time to check gauge.

Pattern Note
Circular needle is used to accommodate large number of sts. Do not join; work in rows.

Afghan is worked in 1 piece with single strand MC; 2 strands of CC are held tog throughout for border.
Side borders may be worked by using both ends of same ball of CC.
To avoid holes when changing colors, always bring new color up over old.

Afghan
With 2 strands of CC held tog, cast on 102 sts.
Knit 6 rows.

Set up pat:

Row 1: K6 CC, join MC and knit to last 6 sts, join double strand of CC, k6.

Row 2: K6 CC, with MC purl to last 6 sts, k6 CC.

Keeping first and last 6 sts in CC garter st, and center in MC and St st, work even until afghan measures 35 inches, ending with a WS row.
Cut MC and 2nd ball of CC.
With CC, knit 6 rows.
Bind off. ■

Autumn Antics Lap Robe

Design by Diane Zangl

THE UNDULATING RIB PATTERN OF THIS LAP ROBE IS WORKED WITH INCREASES AND DECREASES TO ACHIEVE THE WAVY EFFECT.

Skill Level

 INTERMEDIATE

Finished Size

Approx 40 x 45 inches

Materials

5 BULKY Plymouth Encore Colorspun Chunky 75 percent acrylic/25 percent wool bulky weight yarn (143 yds/100g per ball): 9 balls autumn variegated #7128

- Size 10½ (6.5mm) 36-inch circular needle
- Stitch marker

Gauge

18 sts and 16 rows = 4 inches/10cm in pattern st

To save time, take time to check gauge.

Pattern Notes

Only RS rows are shown on chart.
St count changes on Row 16,
then returns to original 18-st rep on Row 18.
To avoid confusion, mark RS of work.

Throw

Cast on 185 sts.

Set up pat:

Row 1 (WS): Sl1p wyif, *k1, p1; rep from * across.
Mark next row as RS.
Work pat from chart until throw measures approx 45 inches, ending with Row 1 or Row 19.
Bind off. ∎

AUTUMN ANTICS CHART
18 sts (shown compacted to 16 squares)
End / Rep / Beg

STITCH KEY

☐ K on RS, p on WS
− P on RS, k on WS
[n] Sl 1 knitwise wyib
⋌ Sl 1 knitwise, k2tog, psso
⋋ K3tog
⋎ Central Double Inc: Knit in back then in front of next st, insert LH needle behind vertical strand that runs downward 2 sts just made and knit in back of this strand.

*Note: Only RS rows are shown on chart. Work Row 1 and all WS rows as follows: Sl 1 purlwise wyif, *k1, p1; rep from * across.*

Southwest Geometrics

Design by JEAN SCHAFER-ALBERS

COLORS OF THE SOUTHWEST BLOOM IN THIS THROW. USE IT TO KEEP OFF THE CHILL OF THE DESERT EVENING.

Skill Level

 **INTERMEDIATE**

Finished Size
Approx 36 x 42 inches

Materials
4 MEDIUM Plymouth Galway Worsted 100 percent virgin wool worsted weight yarn (210 yds/100g per ball): 2 balls each caramel #60 (MC), dark teal #131 (A), grape #132 (B) and rust #102 (C)
- Size 7 (4.5mm) 30-inch circular needle or size needed to obtain gauge

Gauge
18 sts and 22 rows = 4 inches/10cm in St st
To save time, take time to check gauge.

Pattern Notes
Circular needle is used to accommodate large number of sts. Do not join; work in rows.

First and last st are kept in St st for selvage. Sections of block are worked using stranded method.

Throw
With A, cast on 154 sts.
Work even in garter st for 1¼ inches, ending with a WS row.
Change to B and work in St st for 4 rows.
Referring to chart on page 130, k1, [work pat rep] 15 times, rep first 2 sts, k1.
Keeping first and last st in St st for selvage, [rep 36 rows of chart] 6 times.
Change to A and work even in garter st for 1¼ inches.
Bind off.

Side Borders
Pick up and knit 4 sts for every 5 rows along 1 side edge.
Work even in garter st for 1¼ inches.
Bind off.
Rep for 2nd side. ■

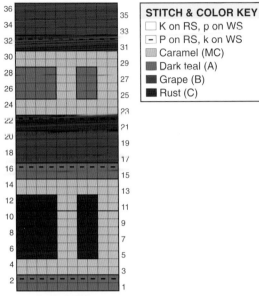

STITCH & COLOR KEY

☐ K on RS, p on WS
⊟ P on RS, k on WS
▨ Caramel (MC)
▨ Dark teal (A)
▨ Grape (B)
■ Rust (C)

**SOUTHWEST
GEOMETRICS**

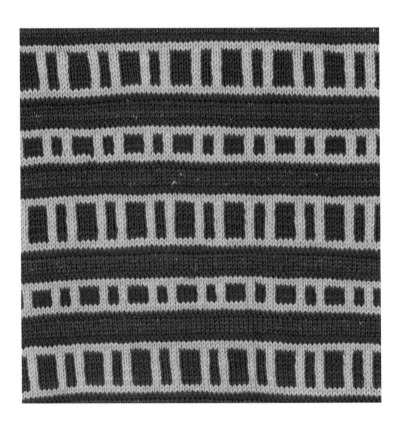

Maple Leaf Throw

Design by DIANE ZANGL

WORKED IN INTARSIA, FOUR MAPLE LEAVES INTERLOCK
TO FORM A CENTRAL MOTIF ON A QUILT-INSPIRED
THROW. DUPLICATE STITCH OUTLINES EACH LEAF;
GARTER STITCH FORMS THE BORDERS.

Skill Level
 INTERMEDIATE

Finished Size
Approx 48 x 44 inches

Materials
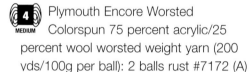 Plymouth Encore Worsted
Colorspun 75 percent acrylic/25
percent wool worsted weight yarn (200
yds/100g per ball): 2 balls rust #7172 (A)

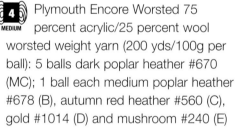 Plymouth Encore Worsted 75
percent acrylic/25 percent wool
worsted weight yarn (200 yds/100g per
ball): 5 balls dark poplar heather #670
(MC); 1 ball each medium poplar heather
#678 (B), autumn red heather #560 (C),
gold #1014 (D) and mushroom #240 (E)
• Size 7 (4.5mm) 30-inch circular needle or
size needed to obtain gauge
• Stitch markers

Gauge
18 sts and 24 rows = 4 inches/10cm in
color pat
To save time, take time to check gauge.

Pattern Notes
Wind separate balls of yarn for each
color area.

To avoid holes when changing colors,
always bring new color up over old.
Throw is worked as 2 panels, each 2
blocks wide by 5 blocks high.
Dark green outline around each leaf
is worked in duplicate st after throw
is completed.

Throw
Right Panel
With MC, cast on 103 sts.
Sl first st of every RS row, knit 15 rows.
Set up pat:
Next row (RS): Sl 1p wyif, k9 MC, pm,
work 41 sts of chart, pm, k7 MC, pm, work
41 sts of chart, pm, k4 MC.
[Sl first st of every RS row and keeping
sts between blocks in garter st with MC,
work even until 44 rows of chart have been
completed. Knit 12 rows with MC only]
4 times.
Work 1 more section of blocks.
With MC, knit 16 rows.
Bind off.

Left Panel
With MC, cast on 103 sts.
Sl first st of every WS row purlwise wyif,
knit 15 rows.

Set up pat:

Next row (RS): K4 MC, pm, work 41 sts of chart, pm, k7 MC, pm, work 41 sts of chart, pm, k10 MC.

Sl first st of every WS row, work as for right panel.

Assembly

Referring to chart, work outline around leaves in duplicate st with MC.

Sew panels tog along long unslipped edges. ■

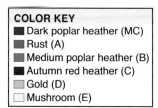

COLOR KEY
- ■ Dark poplar heather (MC)
- ■ Rust (A)
- ■ Medium poplar heather (B)
- ■ Autumn red heather (C)
- ☐ Gold (D)
- ☐ Mushroom (E)

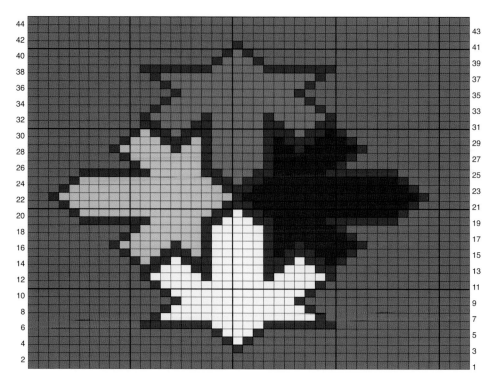

MAPLE LEAVES CHART

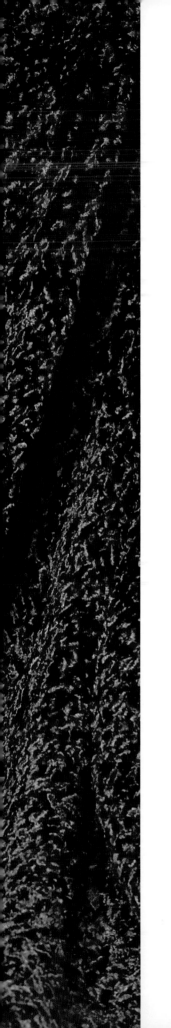

Midnight Velvet Lap Robe

Design by FRANCES HUGHES

A RICH, VELVETY YARN AND OPULENT COLOR COMBINE TO FORM A LAP ROBE OF LUXURIOUS DISTINCTION.

Skill Level

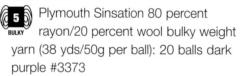 **EASY**

Finished Size

Approx 35 x 45 inches

Materials

 Plymouth Sinsation 80 percent rayon/20 percent wool bulky weight yarn (38 yds/50g per ball): 20 balls dark purple #3373
- Size 10 (6mm) 30-inch circular needle or size needed to obtain gauge

Gauge

10 sts and 16 rows = 4 inches/10cm in pat st
To save time, take time to check gauge.

Special Abbreviation

Psso2: Pass sl st over both the knit st and the yo.

Pattern Notes

Circular needle is used to accommodate large number of sts. Do not join; work in rows.
Sl all sts purlwise.
No blocking is necessary with this yarn.

Lap Robe

Cast on 110 sts.
Knit 4 rows.

Begin pat:

Row 1 (RS): K3, *[sl 1, k1, yo, psso2] 4 times, k8; rep from * 5 times, *[sl 1, k1, yo, psso2] 4 times, k3.

Row 2 and all WS rows: K3, purl to last 3 sts, k3.

Rows 3–12: Rep Rows 1 and 2.

Row 13: K11, *[sl 1, k1, yo, psso2] 4 times, k8; rep from * 5 times, k3.

Row 14: Rep Row 2.

Row 15 – 24: Rep Rows 13 and 14.

[Rep Rows 1–24] 8 times, rep Rows 1–12 once.

Knit 4 rows.

Bind off. ■

Fan Lace

Design by KATHARINE HUNT

LACE AREAS INTERCHANGE WITH SOLID TO CREATE A DELICATE LAP ROBE.

Skill Level

 EASY

Finished Size
Approx 38 x 46 inches

Materials
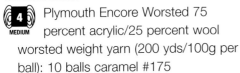 Plymouth Encore Worsted 75 percent acrylic/25 percent wool worsted weight yarn (200 yds/100g per ball): 10 balls caramel #175
- Size 6 (4mm) 30-inch circular needle or size needed to obtain gauge

Gauge
24 sts and 30 rows = 4 inches/10cm in pat st
To save time, take time to check gauge.

Pattern Stitch
Fan
Row 1 (RS): Purl.
Row 2: Knit.
Row 3: K2, *k1, yo, k8, sl 1, k2tog, psso, k8, yo; rep from *, end last rep k3.
Row 4 and all WS rows through Row 18: Purl.
Row 5: K2, *k2, yo, k7, sl 1, k2tog, psso, k7, yo, k1; rep from *, end last rep k3.
Row 7: K2, k2tog, *yo, k1, yo, k6, sl 1, k2tog, psso, k6, yo, k1, yo, sl 1, k2tog, psso; rep from * to last 4 sts, end last rep yo, ssk, k2 instead of yo, sl 1, k2tog, psso.
Row 9: K2, *k4, yo, k5, sl 1, k2tog, psso, k5, yo, k3; rep from *, end last rep k3.
Row 11: K2, *k1, yo, sl 1, k2tog, psso, yo,

k1, yo, k4, sl 1, k2tog, psso, k4, yo, k1, yo, sl 1, k2tog, psso, yo; rep from *, end last rep k3.
Row 13: K2, *k6, yo, k3, sl 1, k2tog, psso, k3, yo, k5; rep from *, end last rep k3.
Row 15: K2, k2tog, *yo, k1, yo, sl 1, k2tog, psso, yo, k1, yo, k2, sl 1, k2tog, psso, k2, [yo, k1, yo, sl 1, k2tog, psso] twice; rep from * to last 4 sts, end last rep yo, ssk, k2 instead of yo, sl 1, k2tog, psso.
Row 17: K2, *k8, yo, k1, sl 1, k2tog, psso, k1, yo, k7; rep from *, end last rep k3.
Row 19: K2, *[k1, yo, sl 1, k2tog, psso, yo] 5 times; rep from *, end last rep k3.
Row 20: Knit
Rep Rows 1–20 for pat.

Pattern Notes
Circular needle is used to accommodate large number of sts. Do not join; work in rows.

Throw
Cast on 205 sts.
Work even in Fan pat, until throw measures approx 45 inches, ending with Row 1 of pat.
Bind off knitwise on WS.

Side Borders
With RS facing, pick up and knit 280 sts along 1 side edge.
Knit 1 row, purl 1 row.
Bind off knitwise on WS.
Rep for rem side.

Random Squares

Design by BARBARA VENISHNICK

GARTER STITCH SQUARES MAKE FOR PORTABLE
KNITTING; A VARIETY OF COLORS IS A SURE
STASH-BUSTER.

Skill Level
 INTERMEDIATE

Finished Size
Approx 48 x 59 inches

Materials
 Plymouth Fantasy Naturale 100
percent mercerized cotton worsted
weight yarn (140 yds/100g per hank):
8 hanks off-white #8176 (A); 3 hanks
each apple green #8019 (B), bright pink
#8018 (C) and coral #8020 (D); 5 hanks
turquoise #8017 (E)
• Size 8 (5mm) double-pointed (3 only)
and 2 (39-inch) circular needles or size
needed to obtain gauge

Gauge
16 sts and 32 rows = 4 inches/10cm in
garter st
To save time, take time to check gauge.

Pattern Note
As these squares are meant to be random,
any color combination that adds up to
16–17 hanks will suffice.

Afghan
Squares
Make 60 A, and 20 each of B, C and D
With dpn, cast on 18 sts.
Knit 32 rows (16 ridges)
Bind off.

Join Squares
Arrange squares in a random pattern as
desired or as shown in Fig. 1.
With dpn and E, pick up and knit 17 sts
along bound-off edge of first square.
Do not cut yarn.
With 2nd dpn and same yarn, pick up
and knit 17 sts along cast-on edge of 2nd
square. Pull yarn tightly where squares join.
Turn.
With 3rd dpn, knit 17 sts of 2nd square;
with newly free needle, k17 from first
square.
Fold work in half, having needles parallel,
both WS tog, and yarn held between
needles.
Insert 3rd dpn knitwise into first st on front
needle, pass it over the yarn held between
the needles and into the first st on back
needle purlwise, wrap yarn around needle
and pull st formed through both sts and
off needles.
*Rep with next sts on each LH needle, bind
off 1 st in regular manner.
Rep from * until all sts have been bound
off tog.
Join squares in same manner until you have
10 columns of 12 squares each.

Join Columns
With E and circular needle, pick up and knit
along long edge of 1 column as follows:
1 st in each ridge and 2 sts in each join.
(214 sts)

Do not cut yarn.

With 2nd circular needle, pick up and knit in same manner along long edge of next column.

Turn, knit all sts of 2nd column onto first needle. (428 sts)

Fold work in half and bind off/join both columns as for squares.

Rep until all columns are joined.

Outside Edging

With E and circular needle, beg at upper right corner, pick up and knit 17 sts along bound-off edge of each square and 2 sts in each join. (188 sts)

Knit 1 row, bind off all sts.

Do not cut yarn, leave last lp on RH needle.

Pick up and knit 1 st in each ridge and 2 sts in each join along left edge of afghan. (214 sts)

Knit 1 row, bind off all sts.

Do not cut yarn, leave last lp on RH needle.

Work rem lower edge as for top, and right edge as for left.

Weave last st of left edge to first st of top. ■

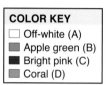

COLOR KEY
☐ Off-white (A)
■ Apple green (B)
■ Bright pink (C)
■ Coral (D)

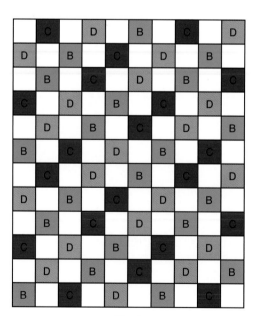

Fig. 1
Random Squares Assembly Diagram

Christmas Stars

Design by DIANE ZANGL

STAR PATTERNS ABOUND IN QUILTING AND ARE EASILY CONVERTED TO INTARSIA KNITTING. THE MARTHA WASHINGTON STAR MOTIF IS INTERPRETED IN A SUBTLE COUNTRY COLORWAY FOR A CHRISTMAS THROW.

Skill Level

 **INTERMEDIATE**

Size

Lap throw (afghan) Instructions are given for smaller size, with larger size in parentheses. When only 1 number is given, it applies to both sizes.

Finished Size

Approx 37 x 40 (54 x 54) inches

Materials

[4] MEDIUM Plymouth Galway Highland Heather 100 percent wool worsted weight yarn (210 yds/100g per ball): 4 (8) balls dark poplar heather #703 (MC), 2 (4) balls dark cherry heather #710 (A), 1 (2) balls medium poplar heather #738 (B)

- Plymouth Galway Worsted 100 percent wool worsted weight yarn (210 yds/100g per ball): 2 (4) balls soft white #01 (C)
- Size 7 (4.5mm) needles or size needed to obtain gauge

Gauge

17 sts and 25 rows = 4 inches/10cm in color pat
To save time, take time to check gauge.

Pattern Notes

Sl end sts as indicated to produce a smooth, chained outer edge.

Wind separate balls or bobbins for each color area.

To avoid holes when changing colors, always bring new color up over old.

Throw will be 2 blocks wide x 3 blocks high; afghan will be 3 blocks wide x 4 blocks high.

Throw

Right panel

With MC, cast on 83 sts.

Row 1 (WS): Knit.

Row 2: Sl 1p wyif, knit to end of row.

[Rep Rows 1 and 2] 11 times, rep Row 1. (12 ridges)

Set up pat:

*Next row (RS): With MC, sl 1, k11, work Row 1 of chart over next 64 sts, k7 MC. Keeping end sts in MC and garter st and rem sts in color pat, work even until 64 rows of chart have been completed.

Beg with Row 2, work 20 rows (10 ridges) in garter st with MC.

Rep from * until 3 (4) blocks have been completed.

With MC, knit 24 rows. (12 ridges)

Bind off.

Left panel

Slipping first st of each WS row purlwise wyif, work as for right panel, having a 12-st garter band of MC at left edge and a 7-st band at right edge.

Center panel (afghan only)

With MC, cast on 78 sts.

Work as for right panel of throw, having 7 MC garter sts on each side of star block. Do not sl any end sts.

Assembly

Throw

Sew 2 panels tog along center unslipped edge

Afghan

Sew 3 panels tog along unslipped edges. ∎

COLOR KEY
▨ Dark poplar heather (MC)
▨ Dark cherry heather (A)
▨ Medium poplar heather (B)
☐ Soft white (C)

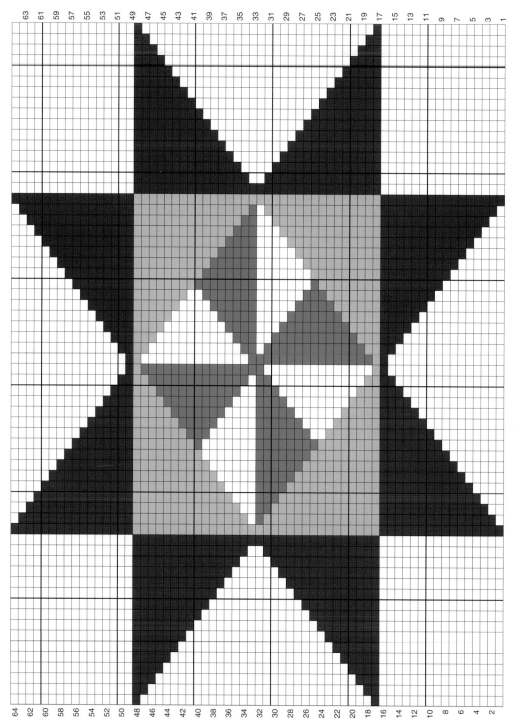

CHRISTMAS STARS CHART

Snow Berries Blanket

Design by DIANE ZANGL

THIS BABY BLANKET USES AN EFFORTLESS PATTERN THAT IS VERY SUITED FOR THE KNITTER WHO WISHES TO TRY LACE KNITTING. THE CROCHETED PICOT EDGING ECHOES THE OPEN WORK OF THE LACE.

Skill Level

 EASY

Finished Size

Approximately 38 x 42 inches

Materials

 Plymouth Wildflower DK 51 percent cotton/49 percent acrylic DK weight yarn (137 yds/50g per ball): 10 balls bright yellow #48
- Size 7 (4.5mm) needles or size needed to obtain gauge
- Size F/5 (3.75mm) crochet hook

Gauge

19 sts and 24 rows = 4 inches/10cm in pat
To save time, take time to check gauge.

Special Abbreviation

DD (Double Dec): Sl 1k, k2tog, psso.

Pattern Stitch

Snow Berries (multiple of 4 sts + 1)
Row 1 (RS): K1, k2tog, yo, *k1, yo, DD, yo; rep from * to last 2 sts, k2.

Row 2 and all WS rows: Purl.
Rows 3 and 7: Knit.
Row 5: K2, yo, *DD, yo, k1, yo; rep from * to last 3 sts, ssk, k1.
Rep Rows 1–8 for pat.

Blanket

Cast on 177 sts. Purl 1 row.
Work even in Snow Berries pat until blanket measures 41 inches, ending with Row 2 or 6 of pat.
Bind off all sts, do not cut yarn.

Picot Edging

Place last lp of bind-off on crochet hook. Work 1 rnd of sc around entire blanket, making sure to keep work flat and working 3 sts in each corner st. Join with sl st.
Next rnd: *Sc in each of next 3 sc, ch 4, sl st in 3rd st of ch, ch 1, skip next sc; rep from * around. Join with sl st. ∎

Bobbles & Lace Baby Blanket

Design by MELISSA LEAPMAN

BOBBLES AND SMALL LACE MOTIFS BLEND IN A BRIGHT

BABY BLANKET

Skill Level

■■■▢ INTERMEDIATE

Finished Size

Approx 40 x 49 inches

Materials

4 MEDIUM Plymouth Encore Worsted 75 percent acrylic/25 percent wool worsted weight yarn (200 yds/100g per ball): 6 balls lime #3335

- Size 7 (4.5mm) 24-inch circular needle
- Size 8 (5mm) 24-inch circular needle or size needed to obtain gauge

Gauge

16 sts and 24 rows = 4 inches/10cm in pat st with larger needles

To save time, take time to check gauge.

Special Abbreviations

Bobble: (K1, yo, k1) in same st, turn; p1, (p1, yo, p1) in same st, p1, turn; k5, turn; p2tog, p1, p2tog, turn; sl 2 sts knitwise, k1, psso.

M1 knitwise: Make a clockwise lp and place on RH needle.

M1 purlwise: Make a counterclockwise lp and place on RH needle.

Pattern Note

Circular needle is used to accommodate large number of sts. Do not join; work in rows.

Blanket

With larger needle, cast on 147 sts. Referring to chart, work even in Bobble & Lace pat until blanket measures approx 46 inches, ending with Row 8 of pat. Bind off.

Border

With RS facing and smaller needle, pick up and knit 191 sts along 1 long side of afghan.

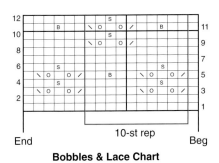

Bobbles & Lace Chart

STITCH KEY	
□	K on RS, p on WS
⟍	Ssk
⟋	K2tog
s	Sl 1 purlwise wyif
o	Yo
B	Bobble

Row 1 (WS): P2, *k1, p1; rep from * to last 3 sts, k1, p2.

Row 2: K2, M1 knitwise, *p1, k1; rep from * to last 2 sts, M1 knitwise, k2.

Row 3: P3, *k1, p1; rep from * to last 4 sts, k1, p3.

Row 4: K2, M1 purlwise, *k1, p1; rep from * to last 3 sts, k1, M1 purlwise, k2.

[Rep Rows 1–4] once, rep Row 1.

Bind off.

Rep border along rem long side of afghan. With RS facing and smaller needle, pick up and knit 145 sts along cast-on edge of afghan.

Work as for long side.

Rep border along bound-off edge.

Sew mitered corners. ■

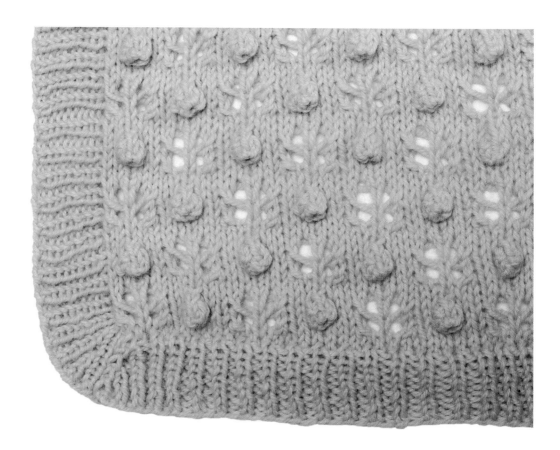

Plain & Fancy Christening Blanket

Design by PAULINE SCHULTZ

A TEXTURED LACE BLANKET IN A WIDE RANGE OF
SIZES WILL MAKE THAT SPECIAL DAY EVEN MORE
EXTRAORDINARY.

Skill Level
 **EASY**

Size
Crib size (small, medium, large) Instructions
are given for smallest size, with larger sizes
in parentheses. When only 1 number is
given, it applies to all sizes.

Finished Measurements
Approx 30 x 40 (40 x 50, 45 x 60,
50 x 70) inches

Materials
3 LIGHT Plymouth Dreambaby DK 50
percent microfiber acrylic/50 percent
nylon DK weight yarn (183 yds/50g per
ball): 6 (10, 12, 16) balls white #100
• Size 6 (4mm) 32-inch circular needle or
size needed to obtain gauge

Gauge
22 sts and 9 rows = 4 inches/ 10cm in Lace
Diamonds pat
To save time, take time to check gauge.

Pattern Stitch
Lace Diamonds
Row 1 (RS): Knit.
Row 2 and all WS rows: Knit.
Row 3: K3, *k4, k2tog, yo twice, k2tog, k4;
rep from * to last 3 sts, k3.
Row 5: K3, *k2, [k2tog, yo twice, k2tog]
twice, k2; rep from * to last 3 sts, k3.
Row 7: K3, *k2tog, yo twice, k2tog; rep
from * to last 3 sts, k3.
Row 9: Rep Row 5.
Row 11: Rep Row 3.
Row 13: Knit.
Row 15: K3, *yo, k2tog, k8, k2tog, yo; rep
from * to last 3 sts, k3.
Row 17: K3, k2tog, yo twice, k2tog, k4,
*[K2tog, yo twice, k2tog] twice, k4; rep from
* to last 7 sts, k2tog, yo twice, k2tog, k3.
Row 19: K3, yo, k2tog, *k2tog, yo twice,
k2tog; rep from * to last 5 sts, k2tog,
yo, k3.
Row 21: Rep Row 17.
Row 23: Rep Row 15.
Row 24: Rep Row 2.
Rep Rows 1–24 for pat.

Pattern Notes
Circular needle is used to accommodate
large number of sts. Do not join; work
in rows.
Knit all WS rows, working double yo as k1,
p1, and single yo as k1.
Afghan blooms by about 15 percent when
washed and blocked.

When joining a new skein of yarn, knit 2 strands tog for 4–5 sts. The slightly heavier sts won't be noticed in overall texture. Trim ends after washing and blocking.

Blanket

Cast on 150 (198, 222, 258) sts
Knit 2 rows.

Referring to chart or written pat, work even until blanket measures approx 34 (43, 51, 60) inches, ending with Row 12 or 24 of pat.
Knit 4 rows.
Bind off knitwise. ∎

Rep

PLAIN & FANCY CHART
*Note: Only RS rows are shown.
K on all WS rows.*

STITCH KEY
☐ Knit
⊡ Yo
◪ K2tog

Candy Stripes Blanket

Design by LANIE HERING

THIS SOFT BLANKET IS WORKED IN ONE PIECE,
ALTERNATING HORIZONTAL AND VERTICAL STRIPED
SQUARES OF STOCKINETTE AND SEED STITCH.
NO SEWING IS REQUIRED.

Skill Level
■■□□ EASY

Finished Size
Approx 31 x 35 inches

Materials
 Plymouth Encore Worsted 75 percent acrylic/25 percent wool worsted weight yarn (200 yds/100g per ball): 6 balls candy #7065
- Size 8 (5mm) 24-inch circular needle or size needed to obtain gauge
- Stitch markers

Gauge
18 sts and 27 rows = 4 inches/10cm in pat st.
To save time, take time to check gauge.

Pattern Stitch
Seed Stitch
All rows: K1, *p1, k1; rep from * as directed.

Pattern Notes
Circular needle is used to accommodate large number of sts. Do not join; work in rows.
On Rows 43–50, make sure to keep Seed st pat in correct st alignment; i.e., knit the purl sts and purl the knit sts.

Blanket
Cast on 143 sts.
Work in Seed st for 7 rows for border.

Rows 1, 3 and 5 (RS): Seed st 5, pm for border,*[k5, Seed st 5] twice, k5, p2, k25, p2; rep from * once; [k5, Seed st 5] twice, k5, pm for border, Seed st 5.

Rows 2, 4 and 6: Seed st 5, *[p5, Seed st 5] twice, p5, k2, p25, k2; rep from * once; [p5, Seed st 5] 3 times.

Rows 7, 9, 11 and 13: Seed st 5,*[k5, Seed st 5] twice, k5, p2, Seed st 25, p2; rep from * once; [k5, Seed st 5] 3 times.

Rows 8, 10, 12 and 14: Seed st 5,*[p5, Seed st 5] twice, p5, k2, Seed st 25, k2; rep from * once, [p5, Seed st 5] 3 times.

Rows 15–28: Rep Rows 1–14.

Rows 29–34: Rep Rows 1–6.

Rows 35 and 36: Seed st 5, knit to last 5 sts, Seed st 5.

Rows 37, 39 and 41: Seed st 5, *k25, p2, [k5, Seed st 5] twice, k5, p2; rep from * once; k25, Seed st 5.

Rows 38, 40 and 42: Seed st 5, *p25, k2, [p5, Seed st 5] twice, p5, k2; rep from * once; p25, Seed st 5.

Rows 43, 45, 47 and 49: Seed st 5, *Seed st 25, p2, [k5, Seed st 5] twice, k5, p2; rep from * once, Seed st to end of row.

Rows 44, 46, 48 and 50: Seed st 5, *Seed st 25, k2, [p5, Seed st 5] twice, p5, k2; rep from * once; Seed st to end of row.

Rows 51–64: Rep Rows 37–50.

Rows 65–70: Rep Rows 37–42.

Rows 71 and 72: Rep Row 35 and 36.
Rep Rows 1–72 once, then rep Rows 1–70 once.
Work 7 rows in Seed st for border.
Bind off in pat. ■

Baby Rainbow

Design by LYNDA ROPER

BRIGHT RAINBOW COLORS COMBINE WITH A
VARIATION OF THE OLD SHALE PATTERN IN
A DELIGHTFUL BABY AFGHAN

Skill Level
■■□□ EASY

Finished Size
Approx 30 x 40 inches

Materials
 Plymouth Encore Worsted 75
percent acrylic/25 percent wool
worsted weight yarn (200 yds/100g
per ball): 1 ball each purple #1384, red
#1386, orange #1383, yellow #1382,
green #054, royal blue #133
• Size 9 (5.5mm) straight needles or size
needed to obtain gauge

Gauge
17 sts and 24 rows = 4 inches/ 10cm
in pat st
To save time, take time to check gauge.

Pattern Stitches
Rainbow
Row 1 (RS): K2, [k2tog] twice, *[yo, k1] 4
times, [k2tog] 4 times; rep from * to last 10
sts, [yo, k1] 4 times, [k2tog] twice, k2.

Row 2: K2, purl to last 2 sts, k2.
Join next color.
Rows 3 and 4: Knit.
Rep Rows 1–4 for pat.

Color Sequence
Work 4 rows of pat, changing colors after
Row 2 in rainbow order of purple, red,
orange, yellow, green, blue.

Afghan
With purple, cast on 124 sts.
Knit 2 rows.
Work Rows 1–2 of pat, change to red.
Work even in pat and color sequence until
8 sets of colors have been completed,
ending with blue Row 2. Join purple.
Rep Rows 3–4, then Row 1.
Knit 1 row.
Bind off knitwise on RS. ■

Dragonflies

Design by KATHY SASSER

SWEET DREAMS ARE SURE TO ABOUND WHILE THESE
MAGICAL, WISPY CREATURES FLY ABOUT.

Skill Level
■■□□ EASY

Finished Size
Approx 38 x 45 inches

Materials
 Plymouth Encore Worsted 75
percent acrylic/25 percent wool
worsted weight yarn (200 yds/100g per
ball): 4 balls white #208 (MC), 3 balls
mint #1201 (CC)
- Size 7 (4.5mm) 24-inch circular needle
or size needed to obtain gauge
- Stitch markers

Gauge
19 sts and 26 rows = 4 inches/10cm
in St st
To save time, take time to check gauge.

Special Abbreviations
3-Throw: Wrap yarn around needle
3 times.
4-Throw: Wrap yarn around needle
4 times.
5-Throw: Wrap yarn around needle
5 times.
Square Knot
A square knot is formed by using 2 single
knots. Bring the right lp over, then under
the left lp and pull up securely and in
opposite directions. Next, bring the now left
lp over, then under the right lp and again
pull securely in opposite directions until a
snug knot is formed between the lps.

Pattern Stitch
Dragonfly
Rows 1–4: Knit.
Row 5 (WS): K5, *5-Throw, k1, 5-Throw,
k9; rep from *, end last rep k5.
Row 6: Knit, slipping all 5-Throw lps from
LH needle and pushing to front without
working. Insert RH needle into each pair
of lps (1 pair at a time) and pull up snugly,
holding thumb and forefinger of left hand
at base of lps, to take slack out of sts
between and on either side of pair of lps.
Tie each pair of lps into a firm square knot.
Rows 7–12: Knit.
Row 13 (WS): K5, *3-Throw, k1, 3-Throw,
k9; rep from *, end last rep k5.
Row 14: Knit, slipping all 3-Throw lps from
left needle, and pulling up snugly with free
needle as in Row 6. Before tying, separate
each pair of lps and bring the 5-Throw lps
up toward the needle. Then tie the 3-Throw
lps over them with a firm square knot. This
forms the body and lower wings.
Row 15 (WS): K5, *4-Throw, k1, 4-Throw,
k9; rep from *, end last rep k5.
Row 16: Knit across row, slipping all
4-Throw lps from left needle and pulling
up snugly as in Row 6. Before tying,
separate each pair of lps, lay upper body
of dragonfly across these and tie this
last pair of lps across body in a firm
square knot. This forms the head and
upper wings.
Rows 17–22: Knit.
Rep Rows 1–22 for pat.

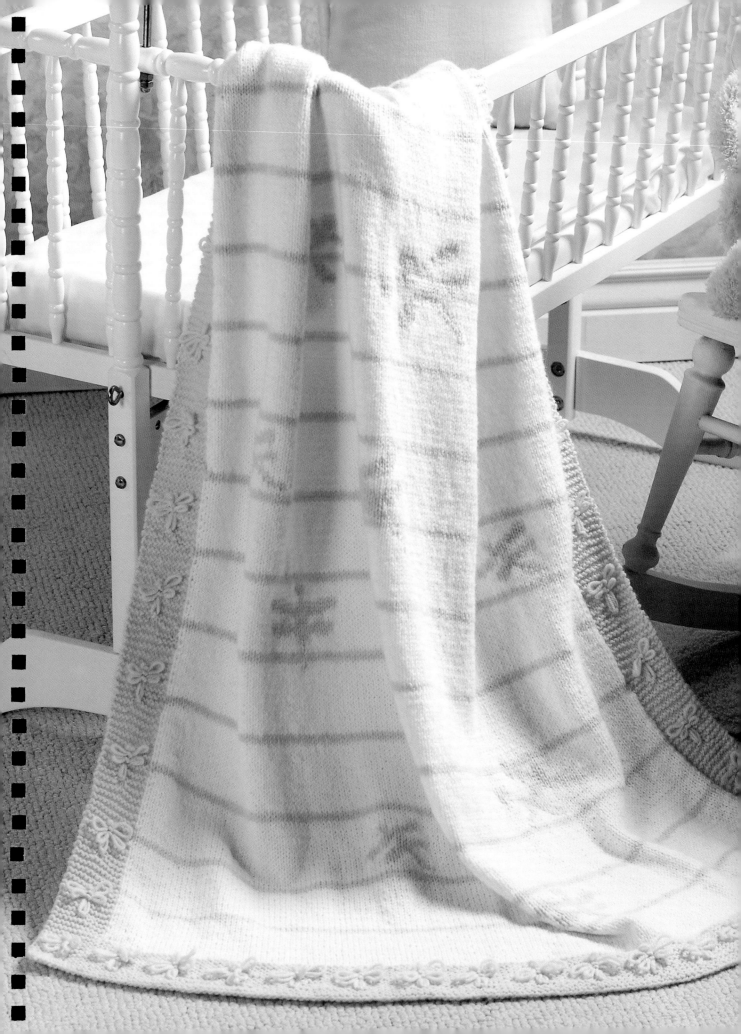

Color Stripe Sequence

Work in St st and color sequence of 17 rows MC, 2 rows CC.

Pattern Notes

Circular needle is used to accommodate large number of sts. Do not join; work in rows.

Wind separate balls or bobbins for each side border.

To avoid holes when changing colors, always bring new color up over old.

Dragonfly motifs are worked at random in duplicate st after blanket is complete.

Blanket

With CC, cast on 181 sts.
Work 22 rows of Dragonflies pat.

Set up pat:

Next row (WS): With CC, work 11 sts in Dragonfly pat, pm, p159 MC, pm, join 2nd ball of CC and work 11 sts in Dragonfly pat. Keeping 11 sts at each end in established Dragonfly pat and rem sts in Color Stripe sequence, work even until 14 white stripes have been completed. Cut MC. (264 rows)
Next row (WS): With CC, k11, purl to last 11 sts, k11.
Beg with Row 2 of Dragonfly pat, work across all sts until Row 22 is complete.
Bind off loosely.

Embroidery

Referring to charts, embroider dragonflies with CC in duplicate st, scattering motifs in a random pat. ■

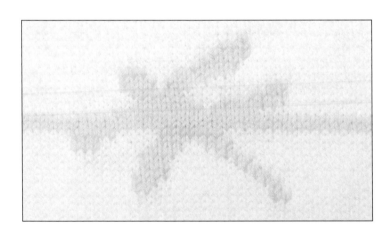

COLOR KEY
☐ MC
■ CC

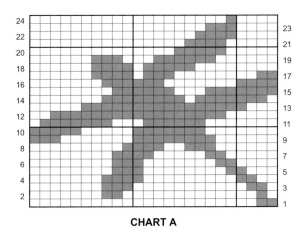

CHART A

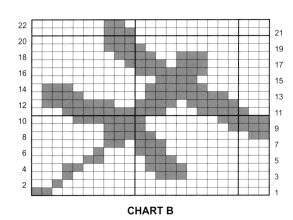

CHART B

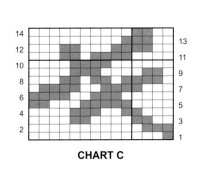

CHART C

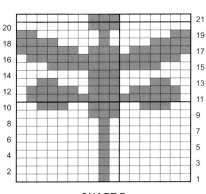

CHART D

Bright Baby Sampler

Design by SANDI PROSSER

BLOCKS IN BRIGHT COLORS AND ASSORTED TEXTURE PATTERNS LIVEN UP A BLANKET FOR BABY'S CRIB.

Skill Level

 EASY

Finished Size

Approx 45 x 42 inches

Materials

5 BULKY Plymouth Encore Chunky 75 percent acrylic/25 percent wool bulky weight yarn (100g/143 yds per ball): 3 balls each turquoise #235, raspberry #137 and lime #3335; 2 balls lemonade #215
- Size 9 (5.5mm) straight and 24-inch circular needle

Gauge

15 sts and 23 rows = 4 inches/ 10cm in St st
To save time, take time to check gauge.

Pattern Stitches

A. Turquoise Block

Rows 1 (RS) and 2: Knit.
Rows 3, 5, 7 and 9: K7, *[k1, p1] 3 times, k6; rep from * to last st, k1.
Rows 4, 6 and 8: K1, p6, *[p1, k1] 3 times, p6; rep from * to last st, k1.
Rows 10, 12, 14 and 16: K1, [k1, p1] 3 times, *k6, [k1, p1] 3 times; rep from * to last st, k1.
Rows 11, 13 and 15: K1, p6, [p1, k1] 3 times, *p6, [p1, k1] 3 times; rep from * to last st, k1.
Work Rows 1–16 once; rep [Rows 3–16] twice. (44 rows)

B. Yellow Block

Rows 1 (RS) and 2: Knit.
Rows 3 and 5: K1, *p2, k4; rep from * to last st, k1.
Rows 4 and 6: K3, *p4, k2; rep from * to last st, k1.
Row 7: K2, *p2, k4; rep from * across.
Row 8: K1, p2, *k2, p4; rep from * to last 5 sts, k2, p2, k1.
Row 9: K4, *p2, k4; rep from * to last 4 sts, p2, k2.
Row 10: K3, *p4, k2; rep from * to last 5 sts, p4, k1.
Row 11: K1, p1, *k4, p2; rep from * to last 6 sts, k4, p1, k1.
Row 12: K1, *p4, k2; rep from * to last st, k1.
Row 13: K2, *p2, k4; rep from * across row.
Row 14: K1, p2, *k2, p4; rep from * to last 5 sts, k2, p2, k1.
Rows 15 and 17: K4, *p2, k4; rep from * to last 4 sts, p2, k2.
Rows 16 and 18: K1, p2, *k2, p4; rep from * to last 6 sts, k2, p3, k1.
Row 19: K5, *p2, k4; rep from * to last 3 sts, p2, k1.
Row 20: K2, *p4, k2; rep from * across row.
Row 21: K1, *p2, k4; rep from * to last st, k1.
Row 22: K1, p3, *k2, p4; rep from * to last 4 sts, k2, p1, k1.
Row 23: K3, *p2, k4; rep from * to last 5 sts, p2, k3.
Row 24: K1, p1, *k2, p4; rep from * to last 6 sts, k2, p3, k1.

Row 25: K1, *k4, p2; rep from * to last
st, k1.
Row 26: K2, *p4, k2; rep from * across row.
Work Rows 1–20 once, rep Rows 3–20
once. (44 rows)

C. Green Block

Row 1 (RS) and 2: Knit.
Row 3: K1, *k5, p5; rep from * to last
st, k1.
Row 4: K1, p1, *k5, p5; rep from * to last
5 sts, p4, k1.
Row 5: K4, *p5, k5; rep from * to last 3
sts, k3.
Row 6: K1, p3, *k5, p5; rep from * to last
3 sts, p2, k1.
Row 7: K2, *p5, k5; rep from * to last 5
sts, k5.
Row 8: K1, p5, *k5, p5; rep from * to last
st, k1.
Row 9: K1, *k5, p5; rep from * to last
st, k1.
Row 10: *K5, p5; rep from * to last 2
sts, k2.
Row 11: K1, p2, k5, *p5, k5; rep from *
to last 4 sts, p3, k1.
Row 12: K3, *p5, k5; rep from * to last
4 sts p3, k1.
Row 13: K1, p4, k5, *p5, k5; rep from * to
last 2 sts, p1, k1.
Row 14: K1, *p5, k5; rep from * to last
st, k1.
Work Rows 1–14 once, rep [Rows 3–14] 3
times, work Rows 3–8 once. (44 rows)

D. Pink Block

Row 1 (RS) and 2: Knit.
Row 3 and all RS rows: Knit.
Row 4: K3, *p3, k2; rep from * to last 4 sts,
p3, k1.
Row 6: K1, p1, k2, *p3, k2; rep from * to
last 3 sts, p2, k1.
Row 8: K1, p2, k2, *p3, k2; rep from * to
last 2 sts, p1, k1.

Row 10: K1, *p3, k2; rep from * to last
st, k1.
Work Rows 1–10 once, rep [Rows 3–10] 4
times, work Rows 3 and 4 once. (44 rows)

Blanket
Strip A
Make 3

With turquoise, cast on 32 sts.
Joining each block to the previous one,
work 1 block each of turquoise, yellow,
green, pink, turquoise.
Bind off knitwise with turquoise.

Strip B
Make 2

With green, cast on 32 sts
Joining each block to the previous one,
work 1 block each of green, pink, turquoise,
yellow, green.
Bind off knitwise with green.

Assembly

Sew strips tog, alternating strips A, B,
A, B, A.

Side Border

With pink and circular needle, pick up
and knit 3 sts for every 4 rows along 1
side edge.
Knit 7 rows, inc 1 st each end of every
RS row.
Change to yellow and knit 1 row, inc 1 st
each end of row.
Bind off knitwise.
Rep along opposite side.

Top & Bottom Borders

With pink and circular needle, pick up and
knit 1 st in each cast-on st.
Work as for side border.
Rep along bound-off edge.
Sew angled ends of borders tog. ∎

Blanket Doll

Design by SHARI HAUX

A BLANKET SQUARE IS TURNED INTO A BEDTIME FRIEND IN THIS CHARMING PROJECT.

Skill Level
 EASY

Finished Size
Approx 37 x 37 inches

Materials
[4 MEDIUM] Plymouth Encore Worsted 75 percent acrylic/25 percent wool worsted weight yarn (200 yds/100g per ball): 4 balls white #146 (MC), 1 ball pink #1385 (CC), small amount black
- Size 10 (6mm) straight and double-pointed needles or size needed to obtain gauge
- Foam ball, approx 5 inches in diameter
- Small amount polyester batting for wrapping ball and stuffing arms
- Stitch markers

Gauge
16 sts and 18 rows = 4 inches/10cm in St st
To save time, take time to check gauge.

Blanket
With MC, cast on 130 sts.
Knit 7 rows.
Row 1 (RS): K6, pm, knit to last 6 sts, pm, k6.
Row 2: K6, purl to last 6 sts, k6.
Rep Rows 1 and 2 until blanket measures 35 inches, ending with Row 2 of pat.
Knit 8 rows.
Bind off.

Arms
With MC and dpn, cast on 20 sts leaving a 12-inch end for sewing later.
Join without twisting, pm between first and last st.
Work even in St st until arms measure 18 inches.
Bind off.
Cut yarn, leaving a 12-inch end.

Head
Place ball in one corner of blanket.
Referring to photo, mark blanket for eyes and mouth.
Using Fig. 1 as a guide, stitch mouth and eyes with black.
Tightly wrap ball with batting.
Cut a strand of MC, 18 inches long and set aside.
Place head under 1 corner of blanket and tie tightly with reserved strand.

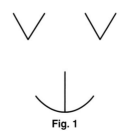

Fig. 1

Center arms around head and knot
very tightly.
Fill each end with batting; sew ends closed
with attached yarn end.
Pull sewing ends to inside.

Hat

With CC, cast on 45 sts.
Row 1: *K2, p2; rep from * to last st, k1.
Row 2: P1, *k2, p2; rep from * across.
Rep Rows 1 and 2 until hat measures
2½ inches, ending with Row 2.
Work even in St st until hat measures
5 inches, ending with a WS row.

Shape crown
Row 1: K2tog, k7, ssk, pm; rep from * to
last st, k1.
Rows 2 and 4: Purl.
Row 3: K2tog, knit to 2 sts before marker,
ssk; rep from * to last st, k1.
Rep Rows 3 and 4 until 13 sts rem.
Cut yarn leaving a 24-inch end.
Draw yarn through rem sts twice and
pull tightly.
Sew back seam, do not cut yarn.
St hat into place on head. ■

Strawberry Stripes Baby Blanket

Design by LYNDA ROPER

FRESH STRAWBERRIES ARE CENTERED ON SMALL

DIAMOND PANELS IN A DAINTY BABY BLANKET.

Skill Level
 **EASY**

Finished Size
Approx 30 x 32 inches

Materials
 Plymouth Encore Worsted 75 percent acrylic/25 percent wool worsted weight yarn (200 yds/100g per ball): 3 balls white #208 (MC), 1 ball each dark red #9601 and green #054
- Size 9 (5.5mm) 29-inch circular needle or size needed to obtain gauge
- Cable needle

Gauge
16 sts and 22 rows = 4 inches/10cm in St st
To save time, take time to check gauge.

Special Abbreviations
RC (Right Cross): Sl next st to cn and hold in back, k1, p1 from cn.
LC (Left Cross): Sl next st to cn and hold in front, p1, k1 from cn.

Pattern Stitches
A. Seed Stitch
Row 1 (WS): *K1, p1; rep from * across.
Row 2: *P1, k1; rep from * across.
Rep Rows 1–2 for pat.

B. Diamonds (panel of 8 sts)
Row 1 (WS): K3, p2, k3.
Row 2: P2, RC, LC, p2.
Row 3: K2, [p1, k2] twice.
Row 4: P1, RC, p2, LC, p1.
Row 5: K1, p1, k4, p1, k1.
Row 6: P1, k1, p4, k1, p1.
Row 7: Rep Row 5.
Row 8: P1, LC, p2, RC, p1.
Row 9: Rep Row 3.
Row 10: P2, LC, RC, p2.
Rep Rows 1–10 for pat.

Pattern Notes
Circular needles are used to accommodate large number of sts. Do not join; work in rows.

Afghan
With MC, cast on 130 sts.
Work even in Seed st for 4 rows.
Set up pat:
Next row: Work Seed st over 4 sts, p18, *work Row 1 of Diamonds pat over next 8 sts, p18; rep from * to last 4 sts, Seed st over 4 sts.
Row 6: Seed st 4, k18, *work Row 2 of Diamonds pat over 8 sts, k18; rep from * to last 4 sts, Seed st 4.
Work even in established pats of seed, Diamond and St st until a total of 17 Diamond pats have been completed.

Work 4 rows of Seed st.
Bind off in pat.

Strawberry Embroidery

Referring to photo and Fig. 1, embroider strawberries in center of each diamond.
Berries are worked in red with 1 duplicate st over each purl st.
Stems are 2 straight sts in green. ■

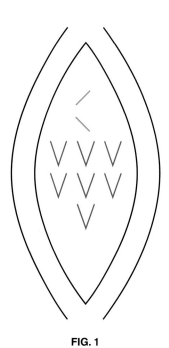

FIG. 1

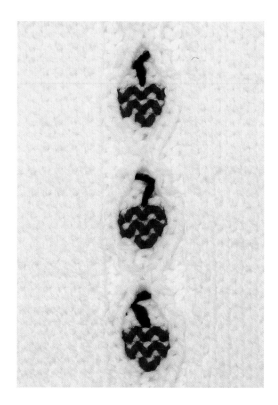

Pastel Pinwheel

Design by COLLEEN SMITHERMAN

THE INTERESTING COLOR PATTERN ON THIS BLANKET IS ACHIEVED WITH SHORT ROWS. THE SMALLEST SIZE IS IDEAL AS A TAKE-ALONG SECURITY BLANKET.

Skill Level
■■■▶ EXPERIENCED

Size
Security (newborn, infant) Instructions are given for smallest size, with larger sizes in parentheses. When only 1 number is given, it applies to all sizes.

Finished Measurements
Approx 17 x 17 (25 x 25, 41 x 41) inches

Materials
[3] LIGHT Plymouth Dreambaby DK 50 percent acrylic microfiber/50 percent nylon DK weight yarn (50g/183 yds per ball): 1 (4, 4) balls lilac #107 (MC), 1 ball pink #119 (A), 1 (3, 3) balls yellow #104 (B)
- Size 6 (4mm) 30-inch circular needles or size needed to obtain gauge
- Small amount scrap yarn
- Crochet hook size K/10½ (6.5mm)
- Movable stitch marker, such as safety pin or split ring
- Row counter

Gauge
21 sts and 34 rows = 4 inches/10cm in St st
To save time, take time to check gauge.

Special Abbreviations
K1B (Knit 1 Below): Knit into center of st, 1 row below st on LH needle. Do not knit st on needle. Sl both sts off LH needle.

Wrap for Dec Section: Bring yarn to RS, sl next st purlwise, take yarn to WS, turn, sl wrapped st purlwise to RH needle, replace marker.

Wrap for Inc Section: Bring yarn to RS, sl next st purlwise, take yarn to WS, turn, replace marker, sl wrapped st purlwise to RH needle.

Pattern Notes
This blanket looks easy but it is actually the most challenging project in the book. Refer to pages 172-173 for help with short rows. Circular needle is used to accommodate large number of sts. Do not join; work in rows.

Blanket is shaped by knitting a repeated sequence of Short Row Dec followed by a repeated sequence of Short Row Inc to shape each corner (see Fig. 1 on page 170). The edge ribbing is completed *at the same time.*

Upon completion, first and last rows are grafted tog.

Pattern Stitches
A. Short Row Dec Section
Row 1 of first rep: Knit until 2 sts from end of row, wrap.

Row 1 for all subsequent reps: Rep Row 11.

Row 2 and all WS rows: Purl to last 7 sts, [K1B, p1] 3 times, p1, turn. Continue working edge ribbing pat on each WS row until sts are taken out of work as short rows continue.

Rows 3, 5, 7, 9, 13, 15, 19, 21, 23, 25, 29, 31 and 33: Knit to 1 st before marker, wrap.

Rows 11, 17 and 27: Knit to 2 sts from st marker, wrap.

B. Short Row Inc Section

Note: *On all RS rows, knit to wrapped st which may have 1 or 2 wraps, insert tip of RH needle into wrap(s), then into wrapped st and knit them tog.*

Row 1 of first rep: With B k2, wrap.

Row 1 for all subsequent reps: Rep Row 11.

Row 2 and all WS rows: Purl to last 7 sts, [K1B, p1] 3 times, p1, turn. Continue working edge ribbing pat on each WS row until sts are taken out of work as short rows continue.

Rows 3, 5, 7, 9, 13, 15, 19, 21, 23, 25, 29, 31 and 33: Knit to marker, wrap.

Rows 11, 17 and 27: Knit to 1 st past marker, wrap.

Blanket

With scrap yarn and crochet hook, ch 42 (63, 105) sts.

Sl back lps of each st onto circular needle. With MC, purl 1 row in crochet lps, turn.

First Triangle

*With MC, [work Short Row Dec Section] 2 (3, 5) times, *at the same time* when st marker is between sts 21 and 22 (31 and 32, 53 and 54), change to A on next RS row.

Continue in established pat until 1 st rem, ending with WS row.

Second Triangle

Change to MC and [work Short Row Inc Section] 2 (3, 5) times, *at the same time* when st marker is between sts 20 and 21 (30 and 31, 52 and 53), change to B on next RS row.

Continue in established pat until all sts have been worked, ending with WS row.

Rep from * 3 times.

Cut yarn leaving an end approx 1 (1½, 2) yds long.

Assembly

Remove provisional cast-on chain and place resulting sts on a 2nd circular needle. With attached yarn, sew these sts to last row worked, using Kitchener method. ■

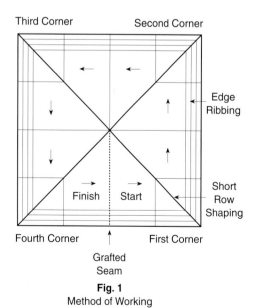

Third Corner — Second Corner

Edge Ribbing

Short Row Shaping

Finish — Start

Fourth Corner — First Corner

Grafted Seam

Fig. 1
Method of Working

Short Rows/Wrap

Short rows add length to part of a piece of knitting. For example, the heel of a sock is shaped with short rows. Or instead of binding off the shoulders of a sweater in a series of stair steps, you can work a series of short rows, and then bind off all the stitches at once in a smooth line. The wrapping technique described eliminates the holes that might otherwise occur.

On a knit row, bring the yarn to the front of work, slip next stitch as if to purl.

Take yarn to back.

Turn work, slip first stitch as if to purl (wrap made), complete row.

To work stitch and wrap together from right side, lift wrap with tip of needle.

Insert tip of needle into stitch, knit stitch and wrap together. (Wrap will automatically fall to wrong side of fabric.)

On a purl row, take yarn to back of work, slip next stitch as if to purl.

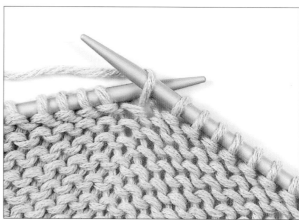

Bring yarn to front.

Turn work, slip first stitch as if to purl (wrap made), complete row.

To work stitch and wrap together from wrong side, insert tip of right needle under wrap from right side and place it on left needle.

Purl stitch and wrap together. (Wrap will automatically fall on wrong side of fabric.)

Close-up of wrapped stitch on right side.

Close-up of wrapped stitch on wrong side.

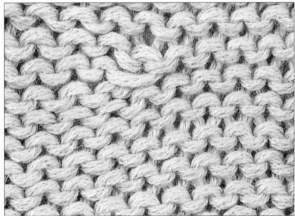

Standard Abbreviations

[ ] work instructions within brackets as many times as directed

( ) work instructions within parentheses in the place directed

**repeat instructions following the asterisks as directed

* repeat instructions following the single asterisk as directed

" inch(es)

approx approximately

beg begin/beginning

CC contrasting color

ch chain stitch

cm centimeter(s)

cn cable needle

dec decrease/decreases/ decreasing

dpn double-pointed needle(s)

g gram

inc increase/increases/ increasing

k knit

k2tog knit 2 stitches together

LH left hand

lp(s) loop(s)

m meter(s)

M1 make one stitch

MC main color

mm millimeter(s)

oz ounce(s)

p purl

pat(s) pattern(s)

pm place marker

p2tog purl 2 stitches together

psso pass slipped stitch over

rem remain/remaining

rep repeat(s)

rev St st reverse stockinette stitch

RH right hand

rnd(s) rounds

RS right side

skp slip, knit, pass stitch over— one stitch decreased

sk2p slip 1, knit 2 together, pass slip stitch over the knit 2 together; 2 stitches have been decreased

sl slip

sl1k slip 1 knitwise

sl1p slip 1 purlwise

sl st slip stitch(es)

ssk slip, slip, knit these 2 stitches together—a decrease

st(s) stitch(es)

St st stockinette stitch/ stocking stitch

tbl through back loop(s)

tog together

WS wrong side

wyib with yarn in back

wyif with yarn in front

yd(s) yard(s)

yfwd yarn forward

yo yarn over

Standard Yarn Weight System

Categories of yarn, gauge ranges and recommended needle sizes

Yarn Weight Symbol & Category Names	1 SUPER FINE	2 FINE	3 LIGHT	4 MEDIUM	5 BULKY	6 SUPER BULKY
Type of Yarns in Category	Sock, Fingering, Baby	Sport, Baby	DK, Light Worsted	Worsted, Afghan, Aran	Chunky, Craft, Rug	Bulky, Roving
Knit Gauge* Ranges in Stockinette Stitch to 4 inches	21–32 sts	23–26 sts	21–24 sts	16–20 sts	12–15 sts	6–11 sts
Recommended Needle in Metric Size Range	2.25–3.25mm	3.25–3.75mm	3.75–4.5mm	4.5–5.5mm	5.5–8mm	8mm
Recommended Needle U.S. Size Range	1 to 3	3 to 5	5 to 7	7 to 9	9 to 11	11 and larger

* GUIDELINES ONLY: The above reflect the most commonly used gauges and needle sizes for specific yarn categories.

General Information

Basic Stitches

Garter Stitch

On straight needles knit every row. When working in the round on circular or double-pointed needles, knit one round then purl one round.

Stockinette Stitch

On straight needles knit right-side rows and purl wrong-side rows. When working on circular or double-pointed needles, knit all rounds.

Reverse Stockinette Stitch

On straight needles purl right-side rows and knit wrong-side rows. On circular or double-pointed needles, purl all rounds.

Ribbing

Combining knit and purl stitches within a row to give stretch to the garment. Ribbing is most often used for the lower edge of the front and back, the cuffs and neck edge of garments.

The rib pattern is established on the first row. On subsequent rows the knit stitches are knitted and purl stitches are purled to form the ribs.

Gauge

The single most important factor in determining the finished size of a knit item is the gauge. Although not as important for flat, one-piece items, it is important when making a clothing item that needs to fit properly.

It is important to make a stitch gauge swatch about 4 inches square with recommended patterns and needles before beginning.

Measure the swatch. If the number of stitches and rows are fewer than indicated under "Gauge" in the pattern, your needles are too large. Try another swatch with smaller-size needles. If the number of stitches and rows are more than indicated under "Gauge" in the pattern, your needles are too small. Try another swatch with larger-size needles.

Continue to adjust needles until correct gauge is achieved.

Working From Charts

When working with more than one color in a row, sometimes a chart is provided to follow the pattern. On the chart each square represents one stitch. A key is given indicating the color or stitch represented by each color or symbol in the box.

When working in rows, odd-numbered rows are usually read from right to left and even-numbered rows from left to right.

Odd-numbered rows represent the right side of the work and are usually knit. Even-numbered rows represent the wrong side and are usually purled.

When working in rounds, every row on the chart is a right-side row, and is read from right to left.

Skill Levels

◼☐☐☐	◼◼☐☐	◼◼◼☐	◼◼◼◼
BEGINNER	**EASY**	**INTERMEDIATE**	**EXPERIENCED**
Projects for first-time knitters using basic knit and purl stitches. Minimal shaping.	Projects using basic stitches, repetitive stitch patterns, simple color changes and simple shaping and finishing.	Projects with a variety of stitches, such as basic cables and lace, simple intarsia, double-pointed needles and knitting in the round needle techniques, mid-level shaping and finishing.	Projects using advanced techniques and stitches, such as short rows, Fair Isle, more intricate intarsia, cables, lace patterns and numerous color changes.

KNITTING NEEDLES CONVERSION CHART

U.S.	0	1	2	3	4	5	6	7	8	9	10	10½	11	13	15
Metric (mm)	2	2¼	2¾	3¼	3½	3¾	4	4½	5	5½	6	6½	8	9	10

Special Thanks

We would like to thank Plymouth Yarn Co. for providing all the yarn used in this book. We really appreciate the help provided by their staff throughout the publishing process. It's been great working with them. We also thank the talented knitting designers whose work is featured in this collection.

Anna Al
Checks & Cables Blanket, 87

Gayle Bunn
Braided Cables Afghan, 40
Guernsey Tweed Afghan, 71
Loopy Stripes, 8

Sue Childress
Blueberry Lace, 92

Anita Closic
Bold Macaw Throw, 26
Retro 1930s Boudoir Throw, 14
Seaside Sunset Throw, 10

Lilliane Dickinson
Cherries Summer, 64

Edie Eckman
Fingerpaint Fun, 12
Snazzy Spazzini Throw, 16

Joyce Englund
Seeing Stars, 123

Nazanin Fard
Funky Foursome, 52

Bonnie Franz
Rainbow Fiesta, 58
Royal Luxury, 62

Shari Haux
Blanket Doll, 163
Climbing Roses, 82
Lilacs in Bloom, 116
Reversible Diamonds, 76

Lainie Hering
Candy Stripes Blanket, 152
Glitzy Glamour Throw, 6

Frances Hughes
Midnight Velvet Lap Robe, 134

Katharine Hunt
A Splash of Summer, 98
Braided Leaf Sophisticate, 67
Fan Lace, 137
Smocking Stripes, 73

Sheila Jones
Funky Flecks Throw, 42
Summer Sunshine, 78

Melissa Leapman
Bobbles & Lace Baby
   Blanket, 147
Easy Mosaic Afghan, 49
Pool Reflections, 80
Walkabout Throw, 61

Carol May
Blue Lover's Dream, 104
Champagne Elegance, 22
Shadow Stitch Stripes, 94

Sandi Prosser
Bright Baby Sampler, 160
Checks & Stripes Throw, 118
Diamonds in Denim, 101
Glittering Cashmere, 28
Long Rib Cables, 110
Slip Stitch Diamonds &
   Cables, 107

Lynda Roper
Baby Rainbow, 154
Luxury Lap Afghan, 124
Simple Sensation, 34
Strawberry Stripes Baby
   Blanket, 166

Kathy Sasser
Dragonflies, 156
Mirror Image, 84

Jean Schafer-Albers
Southwest Geometrics, 128

Pauline Schultz
Plain & Fancy Christening
   Blanket, 149

Colleen Smitherman
Pastel Pinwheel, 169
Reversible Riot of Color, 113

Scarlet Taylor
Rainbow Squares, 90

Kennita Tully
Alpaca Jewels, 18
Complementary Geometrics, 44

JoAnne Turcotte
Party Swirls, 24
Sawtooth Stripes, 20

Barbara Venishnick
Park Avenue, 46
Random Squares, 138
Spiral Paths, 36

Lois S. Young
Contemporary Checks, 31
Serene Seas, 96
Velvet Stripes Lap Robe, 121

Diane Zangl
Autumn Antics Lap Robe, 126
Christmas Stars, 141
Maple Leaf Throw, 131
Monet Miters Throw, 55
Snow Berries Blanket, 144